LEGAL ISSUES AND THE SELF-MANAGING SCHOOL

Issues in School Management Series

Marketing the Secondary School by Brent Davis and Linda Ellison
School Development Planning by Brent Davis and Linda Ellison
Managing Quality in Schools by John West-Burnham
Teacher Appraisal: survival and beyond by Horace Bennett
Developing Your Career in Education Management by Angela Thody
Inspection: a preparation guide for schools by Michael Ormston and Marian Shaw

LEGAL ISSUES AND THE SELF-MANAGING SCHOOL

by

Neil Adams

iv   Legal issues and the self-managing school

Published by Longman Information and Reference,
Longman Group UK Ltd, 6th Floor, Westgate House, The High,
Harlow, Essex CM20 1YR, England and Associated Companies
throughout the world.

© Longman Group UK Ltd 1993

All rights reserved. No part of this publication may be reproduced, stored in a retrieval
system, or transmitted in any form or by any means, electronic, mechanical,
photocopying, recording or otherwise, without the prior permission of the Copyright
owner or a licence permitting restricted copying issued by the Copyright Licensing
Agency Ltd., 90 Tottenham Court Road, London W1P 9HE.

A catalogue record for this book is available from The British Library

ISBN 0-582-22867-0

Typeset by Anglia Photoset Ltd,
34A St Botolphs Church Walk, St Botolphs Street,
Colchester, Essex CO2 7EA.
Printed in Great Britain by Redwood Books
Trowbridge, Wiltshire

For Nicole, Rebecca, Anna,
Katryn and Louise
who will soon be on the registers.

Contents

Preface		ix
1	Finding the law	1
2	Areas of law	10
3	Power to make decisions	19
4	Governing bodies	25
5	Staffing — appointments and conditions	39
6	Staffing — discrimination, discipline and grievances	49
7	Dismissal, tribunals and remedies	60
8	Parental duties	67
9	Parental rights	74
10	Pastoral care and discipline	81
11	Supervision and negligence	97
12	Premises and health and safety	106
13	Financial matters	120
14	Records, references and copyright	128
Further reading		138
Addresses		140
Index		142

Preface

What is a 'self-managing' school? It is one which has full powers of control over its finance, staffing and general conduct, and is subject only to the law of the land and the legitimate expectations of its pupils, staff and parents. Grant-maintained and aided schools are already in that position. County and voluntary schools have gone a long way towards it with their delegated powers and, once the new Education Act comes into force, they will also be self-managing in an almost total sense.

The position then will be that all schools will be incorporated, that is they will have a separate legal identity. They will not only have control over finance and other matters but they will be able to sue, and be sued, and make their own contracts. The governing body, or the trustees in some cases, will be in full charge and recognised as being so in the eyes of the law.

This brings freedom but it also brings responsibilities. No longer will governors and heads be able to blame LEAs when things go wrong, and no longer will they be able to pass on most issues to the LEA for solution. If a school is to be self-managing then it must manage its own problems.

Many of these problems will have legal implications, and this book is written with the aim of assisting heads and governors to understand the law and its relevance to their activities. Therefore, as far as possible, I have tried to apply the law to real situations that could have occurred, and in many cases have indeed done so, in schools.

This is not intended to be simply a book of reference, space would not permit that anyway. It is intended to apply an awareness of the law to the prevention of harm or confrontation and the speedy solution of crises that do arise.

Any errors that have occurred here are entirely my own, but readers do need to remember that the law is constantly changing, even if only to a minor degree.

1 Finding the law

The law is sometimes described as a minefield. If that means that you should avoid becoming involved with it wherever possible then that is good advice. A more appropriate metaphor, however, might be a comparison with a difficult terrain where an awareness of problems to be faced, an understanding of information available and maps to be used and forward planning to deal with possible emergencies are all advisable.

If you fall foul of the law, you may be unlucky enough to be in the wrong place at the wrong time. Otherwise it will certainly be because of thoughtlessness, lack of understanding, hasty action, or a failure to carry out research or take advice. The basic approach to dealing with legal problems that may occur in a school is an awareness of how to discover the law that applies and interpret it in terms of the particular difficulty. How is this to be achieved?

Suppose you are faced with this problem:

Mary Martin

Mary Martin, aged thirteen, is frequently late for school — sometimes as much as half an hour — but she rarely misses a complete session. The reasons she gives are somewhat vague but there is a suspicion that she is being used by her mother to carry out household chores (mother starts work early as an office cleaner) and then to take a younger child to school. The primary school has confirmed that Mary has been seen outside the school gates in the morning, and that her younger brother is often a few minutes late. The education welfare officer has visited the home and has pointed out to Mrs Martin the need for Mary to attend school on time. She has responded by saying that she is doing her best to bring up two children on her own since her husband walked out, she needs the money from her job and Mary's help is essential. The welfare officer has been sympathetic but firm and insists that Mary must attend on time if she is to benefit from her education. *. . . continued*

2 Legal issues and the self-managing school

> *Mary Martin continued* . . .
>
> Somewhat reluctantly the mother promises to co-operate but the lateness continues as before. A warning letter has been sent from the school. Further visits from the welfare officer have produced no improvement, and those of a social worker have been equally unsuccessful.
>
> Mary's form tutor is becoming angry at the lack of action and at the bad example being set to the rest of the class who now consider the matter a joke and raise a cheer when Mary does arrive.
>
> Sympathy, advice and warnings seem to have failed, so further action has to be taken. What is the position in law?

Act of Parliament

Education Act 1944, S.36

> It shall be the duty of the parent of every child of compulsory school age to cause him to receive efficient full-time education suitable to his age, ability, and aptitude (and to any special educational needs he may have) either by regular attendance at school or otherwise.

This applies to both boys and girls of course. The item in brackets was added by the 1981 Act. We see that the responsibility for seeing that a child is educated lies with the parents. Unless they provide education by private means, they must send the child to school and the attendance must be regular.

S.37 of the same Act makes it an offence not to comply with the requirements of S.36. Since the introduction of The Children Act 1989 there are various options open to the courts in dealing with parents who are in breach, and these will be dealt with later in this book.

Statutory instruments

Education (Pupils' Attendance) Regulations 1991

This instrument makes changes to earlier ones, in particular the Pupils' Registration Regulations 1956, and is followed by a circular giving advice on its implementation. There is further emphasis on the responsibility of parents, the need for regular attendance, and the need for schools to keep accurate records and take appropriate action.

Finding the law

Legislation will leave a number of questions unanswered. Here we could ask what constitutes 'attendance'. Does this mean a complete presence for each session? What amounts to 'regular' attendance? What is the position if a parent deliberately keeps a child away because of some disagreement, e.g. over a punishment? What if a parent sends a child to school but the child refuses to enter or runs away during a session?

Case law

Light may eventually be provided on such difficulties by the operation of case law. In Mary Martin's case the decisions in the following will be of help:

Jenkins v Howells 1949

The parents of a child who fails to attend school regularly are guilty of an offence unless the absence is due to the child's own sickness or some unavoidable cause. That cause must be in relation to the child herself not to others. In this case the mother was an invalid, and the child had been kept at home to look after her.

Hinchley v Rankin 1961

Regular attendance means attendance before the official closing of the school register. Attendance after that is a technical absence. The case allowed a prosecution of the parents of a child who was habitually late.

Crump v Gilmore 1969

Failing to send a child to school is an absolute offence, i.e. the prosecution does not have to prove an intent to break the law. This means that, even if parents are willing to send a child to school, they may still be prosecuted if the child refuses to attend or runs away.

Other cases decide that keeping a child away because of disagreement over school rules or school punishments does not amount to reasonable cause.

Department for Education circulars

The law stated above is explained and commented upon in a circular from the DFE. It gives advice on such matters as recording attendance, dealing with truancy, authorised absence, the computerisation of records and legal sanctions that are available. It suggests codes to be used in registers. S.40 is of relevance to Mary Martin:

4 Legal issues and the self-managing school

As to those pupils who miss registration through lateness, the Court's decision in *Hinchley v Rankin* (1961) suggests that repeated absences at the beginning of a session can amount to failure to attend regularly for the purposes of S.39 of the Education Act 1944. Schools should determine a reasonable period for keeping open their attendance registers at each session, having regard to their particular circumstances, and develop firm policies for dealing with lateness so as to avoid the risk of the pupils concerned slipping into a pattern of poor attendance.

From all this we can now deduce:

- Mrs Martin has a legal duty to see that Mary is educated.
- This entails either private education or regular attendance at school.
- Mary is on the register but is not attending school regularly since lateness does not constitute attendance.
- If all efforts fail to solve the problem Mrs Martin may be prosecuted or other legal measures taken for Mary's welfare.

Acts of Parliament

Readers will understand the nature of these. An Act of Parliament comes about as a result of an election manifesto, Government initiative or because of the pressure of public opinion. It is important to remember that an Act only becomes law after it has been passed by both Houses and received the Royal Assent, so details in a White Paper or draft Bill should never be taken as legally binding — they may never become law. Readers may well remember in the past the House of Lords defeating the Government over matters relating to sex education and the restriction of corporal punishment. And, unless expressly stated, an Act is never retrospective. Some of its detail may never be implemented.

The language used is cumbersome, convoluted and technical. This and the use of sections, sub-sections and sub-sub-sections can make interpretation difficult. The reason is that the draftsman is endeavouring to cover every eventuality and avoid ambiguity. A worthy aim but an impossible one and the pressure to produce enactments in a more digestible form is growing.

Much of the 1944 Act is still in force, or has only been amended slightly by succeeding Acts but, since 1980, there has been a series of important ones affecting schools. These are as follows:

Education Act 1980

This Act ensures that each school has a governing body which

Finding the law

includes elected teachers and parents. It requires certain basic information regarding schools to be given to parents. It widens parental choice and enforces the establishment of appeals committees over parental choice of school.

Education Act 1981

This attempts to define special educational needs and enables LEAs to assess those needs and make a statement regarding them. The LEA must then provide the help proposed in the statement. Parents have a right of appeal against the statement. Schools themselves must provide help within their own resources for those pupils with less severe special educational needs.

Education (No 2) Act 1986

This enforces the creation of new Instruments and Articles of Government (see below) for each school and gives wider representation by teachers, parents and members of the community generally. Governing bodies are given powers over finance, staffing, curriculum, premises, discipline and exclusion of pupils. They must provide an annual report for parents and hold an annual parents' meeting. Corporal punishment is abolished, and restrictions are laid down regarding sex education and the handling of political issues in schools.

Education Act 1988

This establishes the National Curriculum, makes provision for Religious Education and collective worship and makes new provisions over school numbers and admissions. By the introduction of the local management of schools (LMS) it widens extensively the powers of governors, in effect making them fully responsible for running their schools. It makes provisions relating to school visits.

School Teachers' Pay and Conditions Act 1991

This replaces the earlier Act of 1987. It establishes a review body to consider the statutory conditions of employment of teachers. It grants extensive powers to the Secretary of State to make orders relating to conditions of service. It allows grant-maintained schools to apply for exemption from such orders and thus create their own conditions of service.

Education (Schools) Act 1992

This sets out the new arrangements for the inspection of schools.

6   Legal issues and the self-managing school

Where to find them

Acts of Parliament are readily available from booksellers or HMSO. Complete copies or digests of them are sent to LEAs and, increasingly, to individual schools themselves. Reference sections in major public libraries should have them. *Butterworths The Law of Education (Taylor and Sanders)*, published in three loose-leaf files contains all the Acts relating to education as well as Statutory Instruments, circulars, memoranda and leading cases. References to particular sections will be found in books such as this one, and in *The Head's Legal Guide* published in loose-leaf form by *Croner*.

Statutory instruments

These create delegated legislation. That is, under an Act of Parliament, power is given to some lesser body to create minor law. Typical examples are Government ministers, local authorities and national undertakings. The legislation must be within the powers granted by Parliament and is subject to scrutiny by Parliamentary committees. In practice, there are so many of these instruments that, unless they deal with controversial items, they receive little attention and pass into law easily enough.

If, say, the Secretary of State for Education exceeded the powers given to him then a judge of the Queen's Bench has power to force him to desist. The same judge has power to compel the Secretary of State to carry out duties imposed by legislation.

It is not always realised that, by means of this form of delegated legislation, the Secretary of State has almost complete control over the National Curriculum and conditions of service for teachers.

Where to find them

The sources are the same as those for Acts of Parliament though they are unlikely to be found in libraries.

Case law

Case law has two main functions. If the meaning of the law is not clear then the courts hearing a case will attempt to clarify the point in question thus creating what is known as a judicial precedent for other courts to follow. If there is no law readily available then the courts in giving judgement will declare it — the rather improbable theory being that the law existed but had never been stated. Thus a court decided

Finding the law 7

that attendance at school means reporting before the register is closed.

Case law then can be very useful in clarifying existing law and filling in gaps that present themselves. Unfortunately, case law is complicated because the value of a precedent depends upon the standing of the court that makes it in the civil and criminal hierarchies that exist. The general rule is that lower courts must follow precedents set by higher ones, and are expected to follow those set by courts of equal standing. Higher courts can follow or ignore decisions of lower courts as they see fit.

The lowest court in the civil hierarchy is the County Court. Above this is the High Court, then the Court of Appeal (Civil Division) and finally the House of Lords unless the matter is subject to a ruling by the European Court of Justice. The only case in England concerning detention as a punishment was heard in a county court which decided that it was lawful but the decision is of little value since the case went no further. A similar case dealt with by a higher court might be decided differently.

The lowest court in the criminal hierarchy is the Magistrates' Court, followed by the Crown Court, the Court of Appeal (Criminal Division) and finally the House of Lords. Magistrates then do not create precedents, but may well pass on important issues for a higher court to deal with.

To make matters even more complicated the only part of a judgement that creates a binding precedent is what is known as the *ratio decidendi* — the legal reason for the decision. What constitutes this in some cases causes considerable argument. We could say that the *ratio decidendi* of *Hinchley v Rankin* is that a pupil who arrives after the register has been closed has failed to attend.

Where to find it

Reports of cases are not easily obtainable. The major law reports such as the All England Law Reports may be found in major libraries but the full judgement is likely to be lengthy and confusing to the lay reader. Authoritative reports are published in *The Times* and some other quality papers and those affecting schools will be reported succinctly in *The Law of Education*. Reports in the *Times Educational Supplement* and other journals are useful but not authoritative. Teacher associations keep track of important judgements relating to schools and should be able to give details.

DFE circulars

The DFE issues many of these but they are not legal documents. In

8 Legal issues and the self-managing school

the main, they give advice as to how schools should implement the legal requirements laid down in Acts and delegated legislation but schools are not bound to follow this advice. Providing they comply with the law, a school's own arrangements will suffice. For example, the circular relating to the keeping of registers suggests a list of symbols to be used. Any school could certainly devise its own code if it wished to do so. However, following the advice is always evidence of acting reasonably.

Where to find them

While circulars may be obtained from HMSO and the DFE itself, it is usual for them to be distributed to LEAs and individual schools. Reference will also be found in publications such as the *TES*.

Instruments and Articles of Government

So far we have explained the law affecting schools *generally* and where this is to be found. The law affecting a *particular* school is to be found in the Instrument and Articles of Government prepared for it. Each head and governor must be given a copy of these documents, and all employees at a school must either be given them or told where they may have access to them. They provide the legal basis for the day-to-day running of the school.

Although the DFE provides models for these documents, they may contain minor variations from area to area and from one type of school to another, so it is important to study those applying locally.

Instrument

This amounts to the constitution of a governing body. It will cover such aspects as the composition of the body, appointment and co-option of governors, terms of office, election of chair and vice-chair, rules of procedure at meetings, frequency of meetings, confidentiality and the position of the LEA and the head.

Articles

This document spells out the duties, responsibilities and powers of the governing body. It will cover such aspects as the general conduct of the school, relationships with the LEA, the curriculum, admissions, finance, religious education, staffing, pupil discipline, exclusions, appeals, annual report and meeting for parents and responsibility for premises. Of particular importance will be statements defining

Finding the law 9

the powers of the head and the relationships between him or her and the governing body.

Summary

The law affecting schools generally is to be found in Acts of Parliament, statutory instruments and case law. That affecting a particular school is to be found in its own Instrument and Articles of Government. Advice on complying with the law, which is highly persuasive though not mandatory, is to be found in DFE circulars.

2 Areas of law

In the last chapter we talked about 'the law'. In practice, there are many different areas of law which may affect the management of schools in various ways. It is necessary to understand the basic nature of those areas and how they may affect schools so that later in this book we can examine in some depth the problems that may arise.

Employment

In modern times there has been a proliferation of enactments relating to employers and their relationships with their employees. These cover such areas as conditions of service, payment, disciplinary and grievance procedures, unfair dismissal, redundancy, discrimination, maternity leave and so on. The law is to be found mainly in the Employment Protection (Consolidation) Act 1978, the Sex Discrimination Act 1975 and the Race Relations Act 1976.

Legal disputes are dealt with by industrial tribunals. These are not courts of law so they cannot create binding precedents but, since appeal from them lies to the Employment Appeal Tribunal, which ranks as a division of the High Court, their decisions are of value in building a body of case law in relation to employment disputes. The tribunals are meant to be convenient and speedy ways of dealing with such disputes without legal formality and the attendant expense. Each hearing has two lay members experienced in employment matters and usually there is a legally qualified chairman. Representation by a barrister or solicitor is not required and union officials are often involved. The tribunals have powers to award compensation and to order re-instatement or re-engagement though these last two cannot be enforced.

Areas of law 11

> **Example**
>
> The head considered that Eric's work as a member of the teaching staff was unsatisfactory. He was sometimes late for school, and his marking of books was often neglected, so that there had been complaints from parents. The head had made his displeasure clear to Eric on several occasions and then reported him to the Governors who decided to sack Eric forthwith. Some of them themselves had received complaints from parents regarding Eric's behaviour.
>
> Eric went to an industrial tribunal who found that he had been unfairly dismissed. It accepted the evidence of his lateness, his failure to mark books on time, and the complaints of the parents, but ruled that the Governors had acted unreasonably. Warnings had not been given according to the disciplinary procedures for the staff, Eric had not been given a reasonable chance to mend his ways, neither had his side of things been heard by the Governors, nor had he been given a chance to appeal against their decision to dismiss.

Health and safety

Although the legislation is closely connected with employment it has virtually become a branch of law in itself and is based on the Health and Safety at Work Act 1974. The law applies to any place where work is carried out, and its provisions are not just limited to employees. Any person lawfully on school premises is covered, so pupils, parents and other lawful visitors are included.

Perfection is not demanded. Employers must take all reasonable steps for the health and safety of those lawfully on their premises. The Health and Safety Commission issues codes of practice on a wide variety of factors and although these are not mandatory employers are expected to follow them as far as possible. Inspectors of health and safety have wide powers to prohibit the use of equipment or practices and, since the Act is a criminal one, offenders may be prosecuted. There seems to have been only one prosecution of a teacher but those of education authorities run at some half-dozen a year. Governing bodies of grant-maintained and aided schools are certainly open to prosecution, and this may well be the position for other schools in the future.

> **Example**
>
> In an Art Department there was a guillotine which had been lying unused in a store cupboard for some years. A pupil found this and used it without permission. The guard was partly broken and the blade slipped, gashing his finger. Hospital treatment was needed.

12   Legal issues and the self-managing school

In this situation the guillotine would need to be removed immediately from possible use by pupils. The head would need to fill in an accident report and inform the employer and H and S inspectorate (the employer might do this). As a result, the school could expect a visit from an inspector. If the guillotine had not been removed, he could make an order banning its use and would probably take the opportunity of inspecting all similar items of equipment in the school.

It should be added that an action might lie in negligence here for the school allowing the possibility of a pupil obtaining and using a dangerous piece of equipment.

Contract

A contract is a legally binding agreement between two or more parties where each gives (or gives up) something of value in return for a similar action by the other. This is a wide area of law and includes contracts between employer and employee and those for goods and services. For a contract to be legally binding and actionable in the civil courts, it must meet a number of criteria.

The basic remedy for breach of contract is compensation in the form of money damages, the cases being dealt with in the civil courts.

Example
The Sir John Falstaff School booked a coach with a local firm to take a party to the theatre at Stratford on Avon. The booking was made in writing and the pick-up time specified. Confirmation from the firm was also received in writing. No payment had yet been made except those by pupils to the school's organiser. The coach did not arrive on time and after ten minutes or so a teacher rang the firm. Only a clerk was available and she could find no trace of the booking or confirmation but provided the home number of the manager. He promised to see what could be done and a quarter of an hour later rang back to say that regretfully no other coach was available. The staff told disappointed pupils to go home and that their money would be refunded.

The important element known as 'consideration' is present here. The school has promised to pay a certain sum in return for the coach firm's promise to provide transport to the theatre. It does not matter that no money has changed hands. This is a business contract and is by implication legally binding. The firm has broken its promise and may be sued for damages unless some amicable settlement is reached.

Areas of law

Tort

A tort is a civil wrong as distinct from a crime. Torts which may concern a school include negligence, defamation, trespass and nuisance. Actions in tort are brought in the civil courts on the basis that there has been some infringement of a legal right. Thus negligence is the causing of harm to others by carelessness, and trespass to land is an infringement of the right to enjoy exclusive possession and control of land. There is a definition in law of each tort and particular defences as well as general defences to tort actions.

The remedy in a tort action is compensation in the form of money damages though, in some instances, injunctions may be appropriate but these are at a court's discretion.

Example

Sandra was an infant. Her teacher dismissed her class five minutes before the correct time. Sandra's mother, who was on the way to meet her, did not know of the change and had not reached the school gate. Sandra ran out onto the busy main road and was knocked down by a lorry.

This was a real case and led to an action in negligence. In a negligence case the court must usually be satisfied that a duty of care existed, that the duty of care was broken, that there was some damage, and that the harm caused was reasonably foreseeable. It was satisfied and damages were awarded.

This case is particularly interesting since, if Sandra had been much older and capable of looking after herself on a public road, then there might have been no negligence. And if Sandra had been dismissed at the right time, and her mother had been late in meeting her, then any negligence would have been the mother's own.

Family law

This area of the law includes that relating to marriage, divorce and the welfare of children. The aspects relating to children have recently been changed and updated by the Children Act of 1989 which has considerable implications for schools. The various problems involving children are being dealt with increasingly by the new Family Proceedings courts where there is an emphasis on informality and a need to do what is best in the interests of the child. County courts also have jurisdiction in family matters and magistrates themselves deal with some issues.

14 Legal issues and the self-managing school

As far as children are concerned, there are a number of measures available to the courts regarding residence, parental contact, protection, assessment, education supervision and other matters, and most of these are now exercised by the Family Proceedings courts.

Example
Harold is twelve and attends Heartbreak Secondary School where he is very unhappy because, he says, of constant bullying. His maternal grandmother, who lives some 50 miles away, spoils him. He would like to live with her and attend the local school where he has friends made during the summer holidays. He reads in the paper of a girl who has gone to court to 'divorce' her parents so he visits the office of a local solicitor and asks to do the same.

Until the passing of the 1989 Act this situation would have seemed ridiculous though actions by minors in the civil courts have always been possible. Under the new legislation, Harold's case could come before the Family Proceedings Court which has power to make orders deciding parental responsibility for Harold (it could be his grandmother), where he should reside and which school he should attend. Any such measures are unlikely here but not impossible. The court must look at all the factors and decide what is best for Harold.

Crime

A crime is an offence against the state and is defined as such in law. The state prosecutes through the criminal courts on behalf of the public though private individuals may bring a prosecution also. The range of crimes is wide and sanctions range from an absolute discharge to life imprisonment. No person under the age of ten years in England and Wales may be prosecuted for a criminal offence and those under 17 are tried in special juvenile sittings of magistrates unless homicide is concerned. Juvenile sittings are not open to the public.

Example
Ben is a known bully and has a quick temper. During a playground argument he pulls out a Stanley knife that he has taken from the art room and cuts Bill in the arm. There is blood and when Bill is sent to hospital his arm needs several stitches. His parents demand that the head take some action. Ben is horrified by what he has done and protests that he only meant to frighten Bill.

Actually, there are two crimes here. The minor one is theft — the dishonest taking of the property of another with the intention of

Areas of law 15

keeping it permanently — of the Stanley knife. The other is very serious even if what Ben says is largely true. It is wounding which is a form of grievous bodily harm for which penalties can be severe. The school should certainly inform the police, and Ben should be excluded as a threat to the safety of other pupils.

Meetings

While there is general law relating to meetings, the law relating to the meetings of governors will be found in the Instrument of Government for each school which may contain some local variations. Unless specifically stated by resolutions of a governing body, other meetings such as those of staff have no legal requirements. The annual meeting for parents has a statutory basis in the Education (No. 2) Act 1986.

Example

There are 12 governors of a primary school including the head. Attendance by governors is poor. At one meeting only four governors attend but the meeting goes ahead and decisions are taken. At the next meeting only three governors are present and, although at the outset the low attendance is commented upon by one member, the meeting proceeds since important decisions have to be taken.

It is normal for the constitution of any body to declare a quorum for meetings, that is the minimum number that must be present for formal decisions to be taken. We do not know the quorum for this group but, usually for full governors' meetings, it is one-third of the membership, or one-third rounded up to the next whole number. Here then the quorum is likely to be four. If that is so then the decisions taken at the first meeting stand. Once the low attendance at the second meeting has been drawn to the attention of the chair then he or she must rule that, while the meeting may continue informally, no binding decisions may be taken.

Copyright

This is the branch of law that protects the rights of creators of original work such as writing, music and art not to have their work copied without permission. It is a form of 'intellectual property' — that is where the property has no tangible existence but is present in the legal right to sue for wrongful use.

16 Legal issues and the self-managing school

Copyright is governed almost entirely by the new Copyright Act of 1988, and the remedy is a suit for damages in the civil courts and possibly an injunction to prevent repetition.

> **Example**
> A teacher wrote a poem which was published in an anthology of verse for schools. A student came to do teaching practice in the school where he taught. Unknown to the teacher she decided to use the poem with a class and she made 30 copies by placing the page of the book itself in the machine. She had a shock when it was pointed out who the author was.

The student was in breach of copyright in two ways. She did not have permission from the poet to copy the poem, neither did she have permission from the publisher to copy the typesetting in the printed book.

Data protection

The law relating to the storage of data is based on the Data Protection Act of 1984, and came about largely because of the tremendous growth in the storage of information by electronic means on computers. It is designed to protect the privacy of information relating to individuals and prevent the possible misuse of such information by others. It applies to storing of data by automatic means but not to other methods.

The Act is a criminal one so those in breach may be prosecuted.

> **Example**
> A teacher has a computer at home and spends a great deal of time playing with the machine. He decides to record the names and addresses of all the pupils that he teaches, and adds the marks given to each for work carried out during the academic year.

This is a clear breach of the Act unless the teacher has registered as a 'user' in which case the pupils concerned would need to have been informed of what is taking place and have information as to how access to the data may be gained.

Road traffic

Readers will be only too aware of the complexities of the law relating to motor vehicles and driving on public roads. The main aspect of this area affecting schools is that relating to the running of a minibus as a

Areas of law 17

school's own transport, the law being found in the Transport Act 1985 S.19 and succeeding regulations.

> **Example**
> Mr Wheel is a motoring enthusiast, has a degree in engineering and likes nothing better than to spend his spare time in refurbishing old cars and tinkering with engines. The school where he teaches has limited funds and would like to have a minibus but it cannot afford to buy a new one. A parent offers to sell his minibus to the school at a very cheap price. It is five years old and has only been used privately for his family.

If the minibus is to be used to carry pupils and no charge is to be made then there is no problem here providing that there is proper insurance, road tax and an MOT certificate. Its use is the same as for a private vehicle. Presumably, however, the school would wish to make charges in order to cover running costs and this creates difficulties. It would necessitate a permit to operate, obtainable either direct from the Traffic Commissioners or through the LEA, and a compliance with complicated regulations regarding exits, seating, lighting, fuel tank and other matters.

Premises

As well as Health and Safety legislation affecting schools as places of work, there are other areas which may concern the use of premises. One is in the Occupiers' Liability Act 1957 as extended by a succeeding Act of 1984. In effect, these put liability for negligence on a statutory basis. Another is the licensing for public entertainment and the holding of lotteries. If a school runs its own meals service or operates a tuckshop then it will have to comply with legislation passed in 1990 relating to standards for those who supply food. The legislation applies to vending machines and food provided at events such as fairs and jumble sales.

> **Example**
> The PTA is holding a dance. It is decided to have a bar serving alcoholic drinks but there is as yet no licence for this and the committee is worried as to the cost. It is also planned to conduct a raffle during the evening.

If the dance is open only to staff, parents and their guests then it will not be a public entertainment so no licence for the music and dancing is necessary. If tickets are on sale to other members of the general public then such a licence will be required.

18 Legal issues and the self-managing school

An organisation such as a PTA is allowed to take out an occasional licence for the sale of alcohol three times in any one year. Licences are obtainable from the local magistrates' court on payment of a small fee. Conditions may be set and the event will be open to inspection by the police.

The raffle needs no permission from anyone, but tickets may only be sold during the event itself, there must be no cash prizes, and all proceeds must go to the organisation.

Summary

Now that schools are largely self-managing units, those responsible need to realise that the law may affect management in a variety of ways, some civil and some criminal. In approaching a problem, it is necessary to identify the particular area of law concerned.

3 Power to make decisions

In dealing with management issues which have legal implications, we need to understand where the power to make decisions in such matters may lie. Of course, in the long run, disputes may reach the Secretary of State who has overriding power in almost all matters to make a final decision, but such incidents are rare.

Here are some statements which will indicate the depth of your knowledge over aspects of decision-making which may create problems for schools:

Questions

1. Another subject is to be added to the National Curriculum.
2. Teachers are to be required to be on school premises 15 minutes before the morning session begins.
3. The allowance per pupil is to be £x per head.
4. Under a statement of special educational needs, a pupil is to be allocated y hours of extra specialist help.
5. A permanently excluded pupil is to be readmitted.
6. Parents from outside a school's normal area demand a place at that school.
7. It is necessary to make a member of staff redundant.
8. A member of staff is to be given a formal warning under disciplinary procedures.
9. Sex education is to form part of the school's curriculum.
10. A county school with a large proportion of ethnic minority pupils would like to be excused from following the rules over the Christian element in corporate worship.

20   Legal issues and the self-managing school

11. Staff in a school wish to see mixed ability groupings replaced by a system of setting in various curriculum areas.

12. A pupil from outside the school's normal intake area has been granted a place. The parents ask for free transport to be provided.

13. An 11–16 school wishes to create a sixth form.

14. A school needs a new photocopying machine.

15. Detention after school is no longer to be used as a punishment.

16. The wearing of jeans is banned according to the school rules, and a parent has complained to the governors.

17. An LEA produces a new Instrument and Articles of Government for a county school. The governors disagree with some of its provisions.

Answers

1. The decision would be made by the Secretary of State.

2. The Secretary of State could make this a new condition in the next edition of the Blue Book but a school would also have to calculate it within the 1265 hours of directed time unless that figure was also changed. The head could also require this of staff but again it would have to be within the 1265 hours.

3. This is the decision of the LEA within its overall budget for schools.

4. The LEA is responsible for the statement and the provision within it.

5. The governors of all schools may make this decision. The LEA may make the decision for county, voluntary and special agreement schools but, if their governors disagree, then an independent appeals panel has the last word.

6. An Education Appeals Committee has the final say and may even override the school's standard number. The constitution of the committee is different for aided and special agreement schools. Grant-maintained schools must have their own arrangements for appeals.

7. This is a decision for governors to make but in the case of maintained schools the LEA must be consulted.

8. This would be the head's decision.

9. The decision is a matter for the governors.

Power to make decisions 21

10. The decision to allow this lies with the local SACRE — the Standing Advisory Council for Religious Education.

11. Unless there are any specific statements regarding this in the curriculum policy of the governors, the decision lies with the head who is responsible for the organisation and delivery of the curriculum.

12. The LEA decides. It is not bound to do so but may if it wishes.

13. The decision lies with the Secretary of State.

14. All final decisions over finance lie with the full governing body. They may well delegate planning of spending to committees or to the head but their final approval is necessary.

15. Unless the governors have given a specific direction, this is a matter for the head.

16. Again, unless the governors have given a specific direction, this is a matter for the head who has the responsibility of formulating the school rules and for seeing that they are kept.

17. In the event of disagreement, the final ruling is made by the Secretary of State.

If you are able to give adequate answers to all or most of these questions without recourse to reference material then you have an excellent grasp of where the power lies to make decisions regarding school affairs. If not, then the following summaries should give you some help:

Secretary of State

- Controls the National Curriculum.
- Makes final decisions in any dispute between a school and an LEA.
- Controls grant-maintained schools.
- Lays down conditions of service for teachers in maintained schools.
- Decides whether a school should become grant-maintained.
- Decides on the closure of a school, the opening of a new school, or a major change in status.
- Decides on extra funding for grant-maintained schools.
- Decides on the recognition of teachers as qualified.

22   Legal issues and the self-managing school

- Rules on teachers who should be barred from employment.
- Lays down duties of LEAs and schools over a wide variety of matters.
- Has overall control of the inspection of schools.

Governors of maintained schools

- Decide on expenditure within the delegated budget.
- Decide on complement of staff and differentials in status and salaries.
- May appoint, discipline and dismiss staff. If they dismiss or declare redundant unreasonably then the LEA may charge cost of any compensation to the school's budget.
- Decide on grievance procedures for staff.
- Create general policies over curriculum, discipline of pupils and sex education.
- May decide to reinstate excluded pupils.
- Decide when to hold the annual parents' meeting.
- May delegate decision-making to committees in some matters.
- Control the use of school premises.

The governors of grant-maintained schools have all the same powers plus the ability to decide on admissions policy, to acquire and dispose of land or other property, and to seek permission from the Secretary of State for a change in status. They may vary the conditions of service of teachers.

Head

- Decides on implementation of the curriculum in line with the general policy stated by the governors.
- Has power to exclude, but not reinstate, pupils.
- May suspend members of staff and give warnings under disciplinary procedures.
- Decides on school rules and acceptable standards of behaviour, though this is subject to the general policy on discipline of the governors and any specific directions they have given.
- Is responsible for the internal organisation and management of the school and so may make a wide variety of decisions under that heading.

Those readers who have been working in schools for a number of years will appreciate how the position over decision-making has changed

Power to make decisions

substantially. Before the implementation of the Education (No. 2) Act of 1986 the LEAs were in a strong position. The overall control exercised by the DFE was couched only in vague terms and each LEA was able to exert considerable influence over the management of schools because it dictated finance and staffing levels. The scope for governors of individual schools to make decisions was very limited. Heads themselves were also restricted by financial and staffing provisions but they did have almost unlimited power over the curriculum and its implementation.

The effect of the Act of 1986 and the Education Reform Act of 1988 was to introduce the delegation of powers of local management to the governors of individual schools and to exercise central control of the major elements of the curriculum. The overall effect has been to weaken the powers of LEAs so greatly that they are becoming little more than providers of services. Governors of schools have gained real powers — and the responsibilities that go with those powers — and central government is able to bypass LEAs and exert its authority directly on schools themselves.

This control and influence has been increased by the introduction of grant-maintained schools which have 'opted out' of LEA control. They are directly responsible to central government. The response, at the time of writing, has not been as enthusiastic as politicians had hoped.

What of the powers of the head? Before 1986, heads were in theory accountable to their governors but, since those bodies had little real power, the reality was that heads were accountable to their LEA. Now heads are largely free of LEA control but they are closely accountable to governors and to parents. We could say that the head who provides positive leadership and who has the ability to work in partnership with governors and gain their trust and confidence is in a stronger position than before. The weak head, or the one who lacks the ability to create and maintain good personal relationships and effective communication, is now in trouble.

Finally, if we examine an imaginary incident, we can perhaps untangle the knot of decision-making that may occur.

Mr Lal

He has a degree from a university in Pakistan and a postgraduate certificate in education plus some teaching experience. He is now a British citizen and has applied for a post in a maintained city school with a large proportion of pupils with Asian backgrounds. At interview, the governors decide that he is the most suitable candidate and decide to appoint him. The LEA adviser who is present at the interview is annoyed because he has suggested the appointment of another candidate of Asian origin who has been made redundant at a

. . . continued

24   Legal issues and the self-managing school

> *Mr Lal continued . . .*
> nearby school. He says that he is sure that the LEA will not recognise Mr Lal as a qualified teacher and will refuse to ratify his appointment. The governors are adamant — Mr Lal is the man for the job. The LEA does indeed refuse to confirm the appointment, saying that it will not recognise Mr Lal as a qualified teacher. He may be employed on a temporary basis on the lower rates for unqualified staff. Mr Lal does not agree and neither do the governors.

The governors have the right to decide over appointments. The LEA can only refuse to ratify if the governors are acting unreasonably, unfairly or illegally. However, the LEA may decide whether a person merits qualified status or not. The basic rule for those with qualifications from non-EC countries is that they must have a degree plus a postgraduate certificate in education, English and mathematics equivalent to Grade C at GCSE, and at least one year's teaching experience. Mr Lal appears to meet the criteria and yet we have an impasse.

When this happens — a conflict between governors and LEA — then the dispute is referred to the Secretary of State who has the final decision over qualified status and any person's licence to teach. On the evidence here, he would be likely to decide in favour of the governors.

Summary

While final decisions may need to be made by the Secretary of State, the making of decisions over the running of schools is largely in the hands of the head and governors at the expense of the LEA. The LEA has almost no power in relation to grant-maintained schools.

4 Governing bodies

In the last chapter we saw a summary of the powers of governors. Now that governors are being left largely to manage themselves and to use those powers, there is a need for their affairs to be properly organised over the holding of meetings and the taking of decisions in a proper way that will stand up to any criticism. No longer is there likely to be available an officer of the LEA to help prepare agenda, write up minutes, give advice on procedure, and advise on general educational issues. Each school will have to employ a clerk — some had to do so previously — and will have to pay for his or her services. Obtaining one with a knowledge of educational practice as well as the conduct of meetings will be difficult. Governors will be expecting heads and perhaps senior staff to offer practical advice on a variety of matters. We can best look at these by reference to a particular school.

The Country Manor (C of E Controlled) School

The Country Manor primary school is of voluntary controlled status and situated on the boundary of a large city. It has some 200 pupils on roll and a governing body consisting of 12 members. The head is a governor. Three governors have been appointed by the LEA which has a Conservative majority, and all are members of that party. Three are foundation governors appointed by the parochial council of the local church. Three are parent governors and one is a teacher governor. The remaining governor has been appointed by the local parish council. There are no co-opted governors. The clerk is a lady who works part-time in an office in the nearby city, and has wordprocessing skills and some knowledge of minute taking and the procedure of business meetings. Her only experience of the working of schools is through her membership of the PTA committee of another school.

There are suggestions that the school should consider applying for grant-maintained status which would have the effect of changing the nature of the governing body.

How governors are appointed

LEA governors are not elected. They are appointed by nomination from the party in power on the local authority. Once appointed they are free to act in any way that they decide but are no doubt expected to follow broad party policies. Case law has decided that they may be removed by their party in power in exceptional circumstances, and this may certainly take place if there is a change in local authority control. Otherwise they serve for four years and may be reappointed.

Foundation governors are normally appointed by the body responsible for the school under a deed of trust which is usually of a religious denomination. They may be removed by the body that appointed them but otherwise serve for four years and they may be reappointed. Ours have been appointed by the parochial church council. While they serve in their own right, there is an implication that they will observe the principles of the deed of trust.

Our parent governors have been elected by parents and serve for four years, even if their children have left the school. Parents cannot remove them and they do not serve as delegates of parents though they have a moral obligation to reflect the views of the parents generally.

The head is a governor unless he chooses not to be so. If he chooses not to be a governor then of course he has no vote but there is a right to attend all meetings except where these are discussing his salary or discipline. The teacher governor is elected by the teaching staff but again is not a delegate but should reflect staff views. The teacher governor and the head must both resign on leaving the school but otherwise the teacher serves for four years.

One governor has been appointed by the minor authority, the parish council, and may be removed by them in exceptional circumstances. Otherwise he serves for four years and may be reappointed. If this were a secondary school then there would be no representative from a minor authority. The additional governor would be co-opted.

Many readers will see that the pattern of governors given above does not fit their own school, for example there are no co-opted governors. The constitution for the governing body for each school is to be found in its own Instrument of Government and this will vary from one type of school to another and according to the number on roll. The main differences from the voluntary controlled school described are likely to be:

County schools

Here there are no foundation governors. Instead, there are co-opted governors appointed by the other governors and they should be

Governing bodies 27

persons representative of the wider community including business concerns or voluntary bodies. Co-opted governors serve for four years.

Voluntary aided and special agreement schools

There is no maximum limit to the number of governors for these schools but there are minimum requirements as to LEA, parent and teacher governors. The foundation governors must always outnumber the other governors put together. Tenure and terms of office will be laid down in the Instrument of Government.

Grant-maintained schools

There must be a sufficient number of 'first' or 'foundation' governors to outnumber all the other governors, and at least two of these must be parents of pupils registered at the school. These first or foundation governors may well include representatives of the local business community. There would be five other elected parent governors and not more than two teacher governors. The head is a governor *ex officio*. Elected governors hold office for four years and the others for at least five years and not more than seven. Again, details will be found in the Instrument of Government.

The main provisions regarding the composition of governing bodies will be found in the Education (School Government) Regulations of 1989. Certain persons are not eligible to be governors:

- Those already governors of two other schools.
- Those in bankruptcy.
- A governor who fails to attend meetings for a continuous period of six months. This does not apply to *ex officio* governors.
- Anyone convicted of a criminal offence which carries a sentence of imprisonment of three months or more given in the last five years. Anyone given more than two and a half years imprisonment during the last 20 years. Anyone sentenced to five years' imprisonment or more at any time.
- A teacher governor who has left the school. This also applies to ancillary staff governors if their appointment is allowed in the Instrument.

Election of governors

This is an area that needs to be handled very carefully by schools when there is likely to be strong local feeling or vying for positions. It is

28 Legal issues and the self-managing school

usual, but not essential, for the head to act as presiding or returning officer, but the responsibility for the election of both parent and teacher governors lies with the LEA or the governors in the case of aided or grant-maintained schools.

Parent governors

The first problem here is in deciding who is a 'parent' as, since the passing of the Children Act of 1989, this could include any person with 'parental responsibility', i.e. natural parents, step-parents, adoptive parents, grandparents even. The school needs to make every reasonable effort to record those who have parental responsibility for each child and any changes that may occur as a result of court action. This is a daunting task. The final decision as to who is eligible to vote lies with the responsible authority — either the LEA or the governors.

The second problem is that of making all reasonable efforts to see that all those eligible to stand or vote are informed of the forthcoming election. The cost of sending information by post being prohibitive, details sent home by pupils may be enough, but this may need to be supplemented by post in some cases. A similar problem exists over ensuring that ballot papers and any statements by intending candidates reach those entitled to vote.

A third problem may be that of avoiding 'ballot-rigging' and a fourth that of deciding on the validity of certain votes.

DFE Circular 7/87 gives advice on the conduct of parent governor elections. A procedure similar to the following would go a long way towards satisfying the requirements.

- Vacancies are notified to those with parental responsibility by a letter taken home by pupils. Where it is known that a child is not resident with a person with such responsibility then details are sent by post. The letter explains the procedure to be followed. A copy of the letter could be shown prominently in school, and a copy sent to any parents' organisation that exists. Transcription into other languages may be necessary in some schools.
- Nominations are invited by a certain date with a proposer and seconder, both of whom must have parental responsibility for a pupil registered at the school. The persons nominated should indicate their willingness to stand.
- Those nominated should be given a chance to make a brief personal statement, limited say to 500 words, and this would then be circulated along with a voting paper to all those with known parental responsibility.
- The voting paper would then be distributed by the same method as before, and should state clearly the names of the

Governing bodies

candidates, the number of votes allowed and the method by which votes should be recorded. It should make clear that the ballot is a secret one and therefore the voting paper should not be signed.

- If there are worries over ballot-rigging then the voting slip could be placed in a sealed envelope and signed outside by the voter. The presiding officer could then check the name against a register of availability, remove the slip in the presence of a witness and destroy the envelope.
- Return of slips should include by hand or post.
- The presiding officer needs to fix a date and time for the return of voting slips and for the counting. An independent witness needs to be present and candidates invited to be present also if they wish.
- In the case of dubious votes, e.g. no X or tick but 'Yes, I think she's great', or exceeding the number of votes allowed, someone needs to decide whether the vote is valid, and that could well be the presiding officer. However, in the event of a very close result, such difficulties may need to be referred to the responsible authority for a final decision.
- There needs to be some provision for deciding ties. The DFE circular even suggests the tossing of a coin.
- Parents will have to be told of the result as soon as possible. In the case of all maintained schools, the LEA will have to be notified.

Teacher governors

The arrangements for the election of teacher governors, or for support staff if that is allowed in the Instrument, should be on similar lines to that for parent governors but will obviously be much simpler. There will be a need to decide whether temporary or part-time staff should be included, and unions should be consulted over the arrangements, though membership of a union should not be a qualification required of candidates.

Committees

Most final decisions relating to the overall management of the school must be taken by the full governing body, for example those dealing with finance, sex education, admissions and the National Curriculum. Those not listed in the Education (School Government) Regulations 1989 may be delegated to committees, though, of course, other committees may be created which will put forward proposals for

30 Legal issues and the self-managing school

approval by the full governing body.

One such committee which will be essential is that to deal with staffing since this will now be the concern of governors. There will need to be one group to deal with staff disciplinary matters and a second group to deal with appeals. It seems sensible to delegate all staffing matters to this first group, the full governing body deciding on overall expenditure on staffing, and the complement for the ensuing year.

While it is advisable for all committees to have clear terms of reference, those which have full delegated powers must have a clear constitution since their decisions could have legal consequences.

The Country Manor School has decided to set up its staffing committee with full delegated powers. Here is the constitution as approved by the full governing body:

Constitution of staffing committee of Country Manor School

Membership

This committee shall be formed by a resolution of the full governing body of the school at a meeting where at least two-thirds of the full governing body are present. At least three members of the governing body shall serve excluding the head, who shall be entitled to be present at all meetings of the committee, as shall the chair of governors. Other non-governors may serve but shall not be entitled to vote. Membership of the committee shall be reviewed annually by the full governing body.

Purpose

The full governing body shall determine the annual budget for staffing costs and the complement of staff, but the committee shall be responsible for establishing pay policies in relation to existing and new staff. It shall be responsible for advertising and filling staff vacancies, both teaching and non-teaching; dealing with staff disciplinary problems referred by the head teacher under the school's disciplinary procedures; deciding on the dismissal of staff in the first instance; and dealing with complaints or grievances brought to them by staff.

Meetings

The committee shall meet as and when necessary but at least once each term. Except in an emergency, ten days' notice of meetings shall be

Governing bodies

given on the initiative of the chair. Minutes shall be kept by a member designated for the purpose or the clerk if available and a report of the committee's meetings given at the next full governors' meeting. The minutes shall be available for inspection, together with the minutes of full governors' meetings, except for items declared to be confidential.

Quorum

Each meeting shall not be quorate unless at least three members of the full governing body are present. However, the committee may delegate powers of making appointments to the head alone or to any three of its members.

Chair

The committee shall elect its own chair who shall not be the head, a teacher or support staff governor, nor a non-governor. The chair shall decide on the agenda for each meeting and shall have a casting vote in the event of a tie. The chair shall decide on matters to be declared confidential.

Disputes

Any dispute over the interpretation of the terms of this constitution shall be referred to the full governing body who shall make a final decision.

Decision-taking and recording

The governors form a legally constituted body and so its proceedings, however friendly, need to be on a formal basis in case any future argument over the validity of decisions should arise. The Instrument of Government will lay down rules over membership, frequency of meetings, quorum and powers of the chair. It is unlikely to do so over the compilation of the agenda, taking of decisions and recording by minutes.

The agenda needs to be agreed well beforehand between the clerk, the head and the chair, who has the last word as to items to be included. A typical agenda might run as follows, and several items need some comment:

Agenda

1. Apologies

32   Legal issues and the self-managing school

2. Minutes of the last meeting
3. Matters arising
4. Head teacher's report
5. Action by the chair
6. Report of the staffing committee
7. Report of the finance committee
8. Supervision of pupils before school
9. Any other business

Minutes

The minutes of a meeting form an official record of decisions taken. They need not give full details of the discussion that took place or the arguments put forward but there must be a clear statement of the motion carried, the names of proposer and seconder and the result of the vote, even if this was unanimous. This may sound to be over-officious to governors used to an informal atmosphere but, now that far-reaching decisions have to be made over the conduct of a school, it is absolutely necessary.

If we look at No. 8 listed on the agenda for Country Manor above, we might find that it was placed on the agenda by request of a parent governor who has received a number of complaints from parents that children are arriving early for school and there is no teacher on duty to supervise. The result of the discussion might have been minuted as follows:

> 8.1 The matter of supervision of pupils before school commences was raised. The head stated that he was always on the premises well before school commenced, and so were some of the staff, but none was officially designated to be on duty. Mr Able proposed, seconded by Mrs Baker, that the head be asked to review arrangements for supervision before and after school and to designate, within directed time, staff to supervise for at least ten minutes before the morning session and at the end of the afternoon session. Parents to be informed of this in the school prospectus, and told that the staff would not be responsible for children arriving before the stated time or remaining on the premises without permission. This was carried by 9 votes, there being 1 abstention.

This provides a good example of a parent raising a matter which the governors decided to take even further. The head is responsible to the governors for the management and organisation of the school but has not given sufficient thought to this aspect of supervision. The

Governing bodies 33

decision of the governors has placed the head in a strong position with regard to both staff and parents.

Head's report

The tendency to produce a glowing report, concentrating almost entirely on a school's successes, needs to be resisted. The aim should be to give governors, and others who might read it, a balanced report on the life and work of the school since the last report was made. This should include successes of course and factors that indicate the well-being of the school as a community, but it should also indicate problems that have arisen, academic performance, welfare, use of premises and so on. The report should indicate those areas where the head has been unable to make progress or find solutions so that the governors can take concerted positive action to deal with them. Many will require decisions which have some legal significance.

Action by the chair

Although overall decision-making lies with the full governing body, or its committees with full delegated powers, some decisions cannot wait for a meeting to be held. Many routine decisions affecting the internal organisation of the school such as those relating to the curriculum, the timetable and pupil welfare and discipline will, of course, be taken by the head and senior staff. There will be other decisions where the head does not feel justified in acting alone. This may be because the issue is a sensitive one or is needed promptly because of an emergency. In both cases there may not be enough time to wait for the next governors' meeting or call an extraordinary one. There may be other matters where the LEA requires approval by the chair.

In all such situations, the chair decides on action on behalf of the governors but at the next meeting reports on the action taken. Perhaps at Country Manor short notice of a strike for one day by some teachers was given under instructions from their union. The head made arrangements to inform parents of the situation, stated clearly those children not to be sent to school and the provision for those who could attend. The chair was consulted, and gave approval, and this was reported at the next governors' meeting.

Of course, if a serious matter arises and there is time to call a special meeting, the chair must do so — usually ten days' notice is required.

Committee reports

On our agenda we have two reports from committees. The staffing committee will probably have been given delegated powers and its report will contain details of binding decisions made, so it will need to be presented formally. The best way to do this is to produce minutes which provide a clear record of what has been decided and which are explained by the chair of the committee. The full governing body cannot alter the decisions made since they have delegated powers — unless by some means the staffing committee has exceeded those powers. They could, according to the constitution given above, change the membership for the next year or even alter the constitution itself.

The finance committee cannot make overall decisions regarding the school's budget so, hard-working and responsible though it may be, it does not have the legal standing of the staffing committee. Though its report needs to be clear and rational, it does not need to be produced in the form of resolutions and minutes unless these are asked for in its terms of reference. Its main task is likely to be the formulation of detailed spending on guidelines set by the full body and a detailed budget for that body to approve. It is only the final decision of the full governors' meeting that needs to be placed on public record.

Any other business

Members of any group can have the irritating habit of raising matters under this heading which cannot be discussed properly because essential information is not readily available. There is a good case for not including AOB on an agenda at all. An alternative is to have a rule in the Instrument, or decided by resolution, that the agenda should be prepared say two weeks before the meeting with members able to request that certain items be included if raised before that time. Only in an emergency, and at the discretion of the chair, should anything else be allowed. This does not prevent individual governors from raising issues but gives time for the head or others to prepare information so that informed discussion may take place.

Withdrawal from meetings

Governors should not take part in reaching decisions which may be to their personal advantage, financial or otherwise. Neither should they take part in decisions which are in the nature of appeals against previous decisions to which they have been parties. In the latter case they should not even be present. In the former situations they could

Governing bodies 35

remain at the discretion of the meeting without speaking or voting, but withdrawal is almost always the best course. Reasons for non-participation or withdrawal are not exhaustive but would include:

- A member of staff whose promotion, discipline, suspension, dismissal or retirement is being considered.
- The parent of a pupil being considered for admission, or the subject of disciplinary action such as exclusion.
- A witness to any disciplinary action against a teacher or pupil. This may be a teacher or other staff governor. The head would need to be present but should withdraw when the final decision is to be taken.
- Members who have been party to a first hearing over disciplinary action against a pupil or member of staff.
- Close relatives of a pupil where disciplinary action against that pupil is under discussion. The parents of the pupil would be present but should withdraw, together with the pupil, when the final decision is taken.
- A member of staff whose replacement is under discussion. A head should certainly not take part in the appointment of a successor.

Confidentiality

There is no legal requirement for confidentiality regarding the meetings of governors, but all members need to understand that they have a moral obligation not to discuss sensitive and contentious matters outside meetings. Any strong feelings that they may have can be expressed freely at the meetings themselves. Statements at meetings will almost always be protected from actions for defamation (explained in a later chapter), but remarks outside meetings relating to the conduct of individual staff or governors may well not have that protection.

Breaches of confidence destroy the mutual trust between governors and the respect they should command in the eyes of staff and parents. Strict confidence is particularly important for those items declared by meetings to be confidential and not available for public inspection — almost always they refer to particular pupils, families or members of staff.

Annual report for parents and annual parents' meeting

Governing bodies are now clearly accountable in law to parents for the

36 Legal issues and the self-managing school

conduct and management of schools. This accountability is required to take two particular forms under the Education (No. 2) Act of 1986, those being the publishing of an annual report for parents and the holding of an annual meeting for parents at which that report can be discussed.

Annual report

There is some misunderstanding as to the nature of this report. It is often written entirely by the head and is a general report on what the school has been doing during the previous year. The emphasis should be rather on how the governing body, including the head, has been discharging its functions and responsibilities. The head as a governor could compile and write the report but it would be much better for it to be prepared by a small committee of governors, and then read and amended as necessary, before approval by the full governing body.

Much of the information in the report will come naturally from the head but there should also be details of the number of meetings held by governors, the attendance record of members, the work of committees, training courses attended by governors, and action taken over important matters relating to the management of the school.

The report must give details of the projected meeting for parents. Governors must be named, the appointing body indicated, and the date given at which their term of office ends. The chair and clerk must be named, and an indication given as to how they may be contacted. There should be a brief financial statement and a recording of any gifts of importance made to the school. Any public examination results should be given and test results under the National Curriculum. The report should indicate how the governors have fostered links with the outside community.

The report should be brief and couched in simple language, avoiding educational jargon. It may need to be published in more than one language.

Annual meeting

The main aim here is to give parents the chance to comment on, and ask questions about, the annual report, so the meeting needs to be held at a reasonable time after the distribution of that report. The governors may agree to invite others to attend as well as parents — teaching and support staff, for example, or members of the LEA or local voluntary organisations. This is not a governors' meeting as such, and so the clerk is not required to attend and take minutes.

Governing bodies

Someone, however, should be designated to keep a record which should be read at the next annual meeting.

This will be of particular value if 20% or more of parents attend — that is 20% of the numbers of pupils on roll. If at County Manor there are 200 pupils, and 40 parents attend then the meeting becomes formal in the sense that any resolution proposed, seconded and carried by a majority must be discussed at the next full governors' meeting and a report on any decision made given at the next annual meeting. If less than 20% attend then governors should take note of any comments made and may well discuss them but are not compelled to do so.

The chair of governors should chair this meeting and may well have to handle it with both tact and firmness if criticism is voiced of individual members of staff. If this happens, and the member of staff is present, there should be a right of reply, if not then that person should be allowed to reply at a succeeding meeting of the governors. Certainly, a slanging match should be prevented. The chair has the usual power to maintain order and require withdrawal from the meeting if that becomes really necessary.

Suppose that, at the parents' meeting at Country Manor, two incidents occurred. Ten parents attended — a high attendance in the experience of many schools — so formal resolutions did not have to be taken. One parent complained that her child in the top class received very little homework. The head then explained the school's policy. The parent replied that this was not working in her child's case. The governors could then thank her for raising the matter and indicate that the school's homework policy and its effectiveness would be discussed at a subsequent governors' meeting.

Another parent said that he had heard rumours to the effect that the school intended to apply for grant-maintained status (see below). Was this true? Some governors had indeed mentioned this informally. The chair could then say that the governing body had not discussed the matter. If that should take place then the views of parents would be sought. An explanation could then be given of the procedures necessary if such action were to be taken.

Grant-maintained status

In fact, the rumours circulating at the Country Manor about applying for grant-maintained status have some substance although no formal discussion or moves have taken place. If that happens then the school will no longer be subject to LEA control. Control will come from central government. The governing body will have to be reconstructed, and will have even greater control over the affairs of the school than its predecessors enjoyed.

38   Legal issues and the self-managing school

The move to apply for grant-maintained status could come either from a resolution of the existing governing body or a petition to the governors signed by at least 20% of parents equal to the number of pupils on roll — in our case that will be 40 or more. This has to be followed by a ballot of parents and an eventual majority in favour. The LEA must be consulted and, since the Country Manor is a controlled church school, so must any trustees that exist and the diocesan authority. Detailed proposals will then have to be prepared on DFE guidelines and submitted to the Secretary of State who will make a decision. Not all applications are successful though the present government is anxious to encourage schools to apply.

The details given here are basic because, at the time of writing, the new Bill going through Parliament sets out to make the process a deal easier than it is at present — for example abolishing the need for a second resolution of the governing body. Once the new legislation is passed, and in force, the DFE will be updating its booklet *School Governors; How to become a Grant-Maintained School* which will give full details of the new procedures to be followed.

Summary

Governing bodies are legally constituted and must carry out their responsibilities in accordance with the law. Most of this will be found in the Instrument and Articles of Government for the particular school which are based on legislation contained in various Acts and in particular in two statutory instruments, the Education (School Government) Regulations 1989 and the Education (School Government) (Amendment) Regulations 1991. Apart from these, governors' meetings are subject to any general law relating to the conduct of meetings.

5 Staffing — appointments and conditions

At the end of the last chapter, we saw the complications that might arise over a staffing appointment. With schools left to manage largely on their own, dealing with staffing issues becomes of major importance so, in this chapter and the next, we examine situations that may arise, explain the law and suggest approaches and solutions.

Case — contracts

A mixed secondary school advertised two posts. The first was for a teacher of history and the second for someone to take charge of a biology department. Applicants were invited to send for forms and those who did so were also sent details of the school and a brief job description.

Mr A was appointed to the history post and near the bottom of the salary scale. His job description had stated that the successful applicant would also be expected to help with a little teaching of other subjects and at interview he had stated his willingness to teach some geography in the lower school. When asked about his outside interests it became clear that he was a games player of considerable all-round ability, but he was not asked if he was prepared to take part in games lessons. In his first year he taught nothing but history. After a year, the school had a crisis in the geography department. To his consternation Mr A found that his new timetable included two classes of GCSE geography and a double period of games each week.

Mrs B was appointed to the biology post with a considerably enhanced salary. Her job description stated that she would be expected to be responsible to the head of science for the management of the biology department. This would include the preparation of syllabuses, ordering and control of equipment and materials, responsibility for safety factors in biology and a general oversight as required of the work of laboratory technicians. Mrs B indicated at interview that she understood these requirements. After 12 months she went to the head of the school to complain that she finds the workload onerous, that too

continued . . .

> *Case — contracts continued . . .*
> much is expected of her in the way of paperwork, and that she is given
> more than her fair share of supervision of laboratory technicians. She
> blames the head of science for this and complains also that he has told
> her to go on a training course for those in charge of departments within
> science faculties. She does not wish to attend and neither does she wish
> to attend the frequent meetings after school called by the head of
> science since this interferes with her domestic arrangements.

The appointments of A and B indicate the necessity of understanding the contracts between them and the employer, and the conditions included in those agreements. The contracts involved are known as contracts of service.

Contract of service

This is a binding contract in the ordinary legal sense but it has special features which are created by the deal of employment law which has been passed in recent years — most of which gives protection to employees beyond the bounds of an ordinary contract.

Whilst under a contract of service an employee must carry out the duties for which he or she is paid in a fitting and professional manner, obey reasonable instructions and act in good faith towards that employer. The duties laid upon an employer are much greater. The employer must:

- Pay salary as agreed and observe agreements over sick pay.
- Observe the statutory requirements of employment law.
- Observe conditions of service as agreed.
- Accept vicarious liability for employees acting within the course of employment and provide insurance.
- Provide reasonable working conditions.
- Permit time off work for public duties.
- Provide references.
- Treat employees with trust and confidence.

These are *implied* conditions (see below) and any subsequent court or tribunal hearing will assume that the employer accepted them on appointment whether they were mentioned or not. Other conditions which are in writing or clearly expressed otherwise are known as *express* conditions.

Apart from those implied conditions mentioned, there is always the question of what else is within the contract and what is not. For teachers this will always include those stated in the Burgundy Book: *Conditions of Service for Schoolteachers in England and Wales* and the

Staffing — appointments and conditions 41

Blue Book: *School Teachers' Pay and Conditions Document* though grant-maintained schools are able to vary conditions in the latter. The details in a job description accepted by a teacher are included and any other matters agreed at interview. Whether the terms of an advertisement form part of the contract has not been tested in law. Any other term added later by the employer is arguable but if it is unreasonable then it is clearly not part of the contract.

Teacher A

He has been asked to do two things that do not seem to be part of his possible duties under contract — taking geography at a higher level than had been agreed, and teaching some games lessons. Perhaps the head had hoped that these would be covered by the general condition of a requirement to obey reasonable instructions. In the last resort only a tribunal or court could decide whether this was so. It seems unlikely. Of course, if the changes had been made with Mr A's agreement, that would be a different matter.

Teacher B

Here the head is in a much stronger position. The job description seems to have been a wide one. Mrs B has undertaken entire responsibility under her contract for her department and, provided the paperwork is connected with those duties, she must cope with it. She must also cope with any workload clearly related to her responsiblity for her department however onerous that might be, and her domestic problems are her own affair. She must attend meetings and courses outside school if she is given reasonable notice and they are in directed time. If she is being given more than her share of the supervision of laboratory technicians, that is hardly a breach of contract but she may be able to take out a grievance procedure against the head of science.

The positions of these two teachers raise issues relating to job descriptions, interviews and conditions of service.

Job descriptions

Many teachers and ancillary staff in post have no job descriptions. If it is desired to give them such descriptions then that must be with their consent — their contracts have already been made. For new staff the job description can be part of the contract but, while the advantages may seem obvious, it should be remembered that a description drawn too narrowly gives the employee opportunities to refuse duties which are difficult to forecast in a complex activity such as the management of a school.

There is a good case for saying that, for teachers without additional special responsibilities, the conditions set out in the Blue Book provide an adequate job description and the same could be said of heads and deputies. Grant-maintained schools may vary these conditions but may well be ill-advised to do so in any great degree. For other staff it will be of value to set out special duties positively, though it should be remembered that a job description is only part of a contract, the employer may still require the performance of reasonable duties implied but not stated in contractual terms — that might just be possible over Mr A's geography teaching in a school crisis.

A relatively thoughtful description of Mrs B's post might be as follows:

Head of biology

1. The holder will be fully responsible to the head of science for the organisation and conduct of the biology department.

2. This will include the preparation and updating of syllabuses, the allocation of staff to classes and general oversight and monitoring of the performance of staff and pupils.

3. The holder will be held responsible for the ordering of equipment and materials for biology teaching, their recording and safe storage and use.

4. The holder will be responsible for safety in the biology laboratories and for informing the head of science of defective equipment, potential risks that may present themselves and any accidents that take place. Details of any of these shall be in writing.

5. The holder shall provide verbal or written reports on any aspects of the conduct of the biology department on request by the head of science.

6. The holder shall carry out any other reasonable duties within the science faculty, including the supervision of laboratory technicians, as directed by the head of science.

This description is reasonably short, avoids narrow prescriptive detail, and gives wide powers to the head of science, who will be responsible to the head for the provision of biology within the science faculty.

Staffing — appointments and conditions 43

Interviews

Governors of aided and grant-maintained schools are the employers, and are able to make firm offers of employment at interview and candidates may give a firm acceptance. Law of contract does not require either of these to be in writing but it is desirable to take this step in order to prevent any future disagreement. For maintained schools, the offer made at interview is subject to ratification by the LEA employer so the candidate is able to withhold legal consent to the appointment until offer of appointment is received in writing and may then decide not to accept. If an offer is made by post then the acceptance is complete as soon as it is posted.

What is said at interview by either side is likely to form part of the contract. The writing down of copious details and statements during an interview would soon destroy the atmosphere necessary for establishing a rapport between interviewers and candidates, yet some written evidence may be needed to settle any problems in the future. The following is suggested:

Before the interview

- Interviewers meet to decide on the basic questions to be put. These questions to be clearly based on the advertisement, any job description given and the specific needs of the school. This would not preclude additional questions that might be put to candidates on points arising during the interview.
- The questions checked as to being proper, i.e. not being discriminatory on grounds of sex or race or relating to political views. Church schools may ask questions regarding religion if they wish to do so but other schools should not though to do so is not strictly illegal in England and Wales.

During the interview

- Ensure that supplementary questions of the type just mentioned are not put to candidates.
- See that specific requirements of the post are confirmed with candidates and that any additional aspects are agreed. Ask candidates if there are any other specific services they would like to offer if appointed.
- Have someone to make discreet notes of essential matters agreed which are not in the job description or in the Blue Book.

44   Legal issues and the self-managing school

After the interview

- The panel makes its decision and puts on record the reasons for its choice. Any matters agreed which do not appear in the Blue Book or in the job description are recorded. If Mr A had said that he would help with games, that would be an example.
- If the post is offered immediately then those matters could be put to the successful candidate. If the offer is made by post, they could be included but pressure would need to be applied to the LEA to include them in its letter.
- The record of the result of the interview, and any special matters agreed, are then placed on the new teacher's file.

Conditions of service

In this chapter we have made references to conditions of service and the Blue Book officially entitled *School Teachers' Pay and Conditions Document*. We need to understand something of the nature of conditions present in a contract of service not only for teachers but for all employed at a school. Conditions are of two types.

Express

These are conditions put in writing or stated clearly in front of witnesses. The interpretation of them may possibly lead to some argument. Express conditions for ancillary staff will almost certainly require a job description. For teachers, while a job description may be desirable, the express conditions may be found largely in the two books mentioned — Burgundy and Blue.

The Burgundy Book deals with employment matters involved before the introduction of detailed conditions in the Blue Book. It includes appointment, resignation, termination, retirement, leave of absence, medical examinations and disciplinary and grievance procedures.

The Blue Book spells out conditions under the following headings:

General professional duties
Particular duties
Professional duties
Working time

There are separate conditions for heads and deputies.

Staffing — appointments and conditions

Implied

It is here that the real difficulties begin. An implied condition is one that is in the contract but has not been stated. The decision as to whether a condition is implied or not will rest with the courts if the issue cannot be settled between employer and employee. The sort of test that will be applied is to ask whether, when the agreement was made, both parties knew, or ought to have known, that the condition was there. If the judge decides that this was so then the condition is part of the contract.

However, as we said earlier, certain conditions are always implied. For employers, that salary will be paid at the correct intervals and that safe working conditions will be provided. For employees, that work will be carried out in a suitable and professional manner, that all reasonable instructions will be obeyed and that loyalty to the employer will be observed. What constitutes a reasonable instruction, or reveals lack of loyalty, are both open questions.

Mr A and Mrs B

Both teachers work under the general express conditions stated in the two books mentioned above unless their schools are grant-maintained and have made some variations.

Within directed time, Mr A must teach history and apparently at any stage in the school. He must teach some geography to lower forms. In both areas he must spend sufficient time outside school for adequate preparation, marking and the writing of reports. It is unlikely that the instruction to teach GCSE geography and to take games periods are reasonable though he might agree to do so.

Mrs B is not only bound by the same general conditions as Mr A but she is bound by conditions clearly linked to the extra salary she receives and her status as head of biology. This indicates responsibilities over and above those of teachers like Mr A unless it has been given for outstanding performance in the classroom or to attract a teacher in a subject where there is a serious shortage. She must attend meetings and training courses provided these are in directed time and take her share in the supervision of laboratory technicians.

Directed time

The new conditions of service for teachers were introduced by legislation in 1987. If we look closely at these conditions, we could conclude that most teachers of any worth were already meeting them and indeed giving far more to the service than was required of them by law. The difficulty was that, over and above the working of the normal school day, nothing else could actually be required of them. Heads were unsure of what they could demand of staff, and staff were unsure as to what they could be forced to do and what was voluntary.

The first really big change brought about by the conditions was the introduction of stated days and hours of work known popularly as directed time. Since this has a statutory basis, heads are responsible for managing this as well as other factors.

In many schools, dedicated professional staff will not be counting the hours worked but, in order to clarify their position, show fairness, and deal with confrontations that may arise, a management plan for time needs to be drawn up.

Teachers must be available for work in school for 1265 hours in each academic year over 195 days with pupils present, and 5 days without the presence of pupils. In addition, they must spend as much of their own time as necessary to prepare work, mark and write reports. That can hardly be quantified.

School managers therefore must budget for sufficient time to cover essentials, leaving enough time over to deal with any unforeseen demands that may occur.

Essential aspects to be covered would include:

- Timetabled lessons and assemblies (morning and afternoon breaks included but not the lunch period).
- Supervision before and after school.
- Staff and other meetings held outside normal school hours.
- Teacher/parent evenings.
- A reserve of hours to be used if necessary.

It needs to be emphasised to staff that activities outside directed time are voluntary — though very welcome.

Appraisal

The second important change brought about by the new conditions of service is the compulsory appraisal of teaching staff which must be in full swing by September 1995. Although appraisal is a common enough feature in many employment fields outside teaching, its introduction into schools has been greeted with a great deal of suspicion, particularly over the use to which appraisal reports will be put and their confidentiality. The greatest worry seems to be that they will be used to influence promotion — or lack of it — and as part of disciplinary proceedings. Some steps have been taken in attempts to allay these fears.

Staffing — appointments and conditions   47

The law relating to appraisal is to be found in the Education
(School Teacher Appraisal) Regulations 1991 and guidance is given in
DFE Circular 12/91 School Teacher Appraisal.

The salient points are:

- The aim of appraisal is to help teachers to realise their
  potential and perform more effectively.
- It applies to all qualified teachers working for at least 40% of
  their time in one school, and under a contract for at least one
  year.
- Responsibility lies with an appraising body — the LEA for all
  schools except grant-maintained, where it is that of the
  governors'. In all schools, governors should be aware of the
  scheme in operation.
- Appraisal must take place on a two-year cycle with a review
  meeting taking place during the second year.
- Appraisal should include classroom observation and an interview. It should cover any job description that exists. There
  should be a statement agreed between appraiser and teacher
  and a review of this. The statement should include targets
  agreed for the teacher's future performance.
- The appraiser would normally be a senior member of staff
  nominated by the head who should be responsible for
  appraising deputies. A teacher may require that a different
  appraiser be appointed.
- The statement made is confidential to the appraiser, the
  teacher, the head and any review officer appointed later. For
  heads, the appraising body and chair of governors are entitled
  to a copy.
- The statement should not be directly linked to promotion or to
  disciplinary procedures.
- There should be a procedure for complaints to be brought
  against the appraisal procedures in the school.

Perhaps the greatest worry for teachers is over confidentiality.
Heads need to be very careful over their arrangements. Appraisers
need to be made aware of the security needed for statements and staff
need to be assured that statements are kept in a secure place under
lock and key. Statements should not be typed up by secretaries or put
onto computers.

Mrs B again

Our Mrs B, the head of biology, will have to be appraised. The likely
appraiser will be the head of science but, from what was said earlier, it
seems likely that her relationship with that person is not of the best so

48   Legal issues and the self-managing school

she may well ask for a different appraiser to be nominated — a deputy perhaps.

If Mrs B has the job description that we suggested then the items mentioned will have to be explored with her. She needs to be asked as tactfully as possible how she feels she is meeting its demands and how she could improve her performance. She needs to be encouraged to air her problems fully and her needs for professional development discussed. Targets for development and performance need to be agreed. Handled tactfully, the process could enable her to take a fresh look at herself as a senior member of staff with extra responsibilities.

Summary

Teachers and ancillary staff are appointed under contracts of service which have legal implications. Such contracts have both express and implied terms. For teachers, express terms are to be found in the Burgundy Book, the Blue Book, any job description and any other clear agreement between the parties. For ancillary staff, detailed job descriptions will be necessary to form express terms. Whether a term is implied or not may need decision by a court of law.

6 Staffing — discrimination, discipline, and grievances

We might have included discrimination in the last chapter if Mr A's post had been advertised for coloured persons only or if Mrs B had been asked at interview if being a mother and housewife would interfere with her additional duties as head of biology. The law relating to it is certainly relevant to both advertising appointments and the conduct of interviews. However, it does apply throughout the course of employment and in addition it applies to the treatment of pupils.

Case

The Blessed Saints RC (Aided) Primary School needed to appoint a teacher. The advertisement stated that only practising Catholics would be considered. They must also be under the age of 30 and have at least seven years' teaching experience. Before the interview the head, not the most tactful of men, was heard to remark that there were enough women on the staff already and he wished to see a man appointed.

Four candidates were interviewed — three men and what seemed a token woman. Each was asked how they felt about working on a staff consisting largely of females. When making a decision, one governor commented that he would rule out one male candidate. This man was a British citizen and properly qualified but was of African origin. The governor felt that he should not be appointed to an all-white school. The other governors refused categorically to consider this as a factor but decided to appoint another white male candidate on grounds of experience, qualifications and outstanding references.

Discrimination

The law relating to discrimination, both inside and outside of employment matters, is to be found in two main Acts of Parliament — the Sex Discrimination Act of 1975 and the Race Relations Act of 1976. The provisions of both Acts are very similar.

Discrimination amounts to less favourable treatment of a person or persons as against others on grounds of sex, marital status, colour, race, nationality or ethnic origin. This may be shown in appointments to posts, terms in a contract, promotion, opportunities for training, victimisation, harassment and selection for redundancy or dismissal. Outside employment, discrimination may be claimed on many grounds, for example, it has been held to be discrimination for an education authority not to provide an equal number of places for boys and girls in its selective schools.

The discrimination may be direct or indirect. Direct discrimination seems obvious enough — a candidate is refused consideration for a post because he or she is white or coloured. Indirect discrimination is more complicated. It lies in creating a situation where it is impossible for members of one sex or those of a particular colour or race or ethnic background to compete fairly with others — an employer declares a policy of making part-time employees redundant before considering those working full-time and there is a far greater proportion of part-time female workers in the work force.

Some actions may automatically be discriminatory. Victimising an employee who has dared to bring an action under the two Acts mentioned above is one.

Some discrimination is not unlawful though reprehensible — asking for political views is one. For most schools, asking questions regarding religious views is in the same category though it may well be necessary for schools with a strong religious foundation. In such schools it would be 'a genuine occupational qualification'. Discrimination on grounds of privacy or decency is also permissible — the appointment of a PE teacher who would be required to supervise changing arrangements for girls, for example.

The remedy for those discriminated against is compensation from an industrial tribunal.

If we apply the law to the incident at the Blessed Saints School, we can see that discrimination is certainly present. The school is in the aided category with a Roman Catholic foundation. It may advertise for Catholic teachers if it wishes to do so and make that a condition of appointment. However, to insist on candidates being under 30 and having at least seven years' teaching experience will be indirect discrimination against women teachers. Those who had taken time off

Staffing — discrimination, discipline and grievances   51

to have children could hardly qualify. The head's comment is clear discrimination against women. It might be thought that the question relating to working on a staff consisting largely of women was discriminatory but, since this was put to all candidates, that would not be so. The single governor objecting to the appointment of a coloured candidate is behaving in a discriminatory fashion but the others seem to have taken no heed of this objection, and their reasons for the final decision appear sound. The coloured candidate might gain some small compensation for the one comment but certainly not for the failure to gain the post.

Discrimination against pupils

> **Case**
> Two pupils are causing problems over their appearance at school. One comes to school with long hair in 'dreadlocks'. When his parents have been asked to see that his hair is cut to a reasonable length they claim that as a Rastafarian it is essential that his hair remains as it is. The second boy is from a Sikh family. He comes to school wearing a turban and his parents are insisting that he be allowed to wear it since that is what a Sikh must do.

As we said, discrimination is not confined to employment matters. If boys and girls are not offered the same choice of subjects in an option scheme then that would be discriminatory. In a recent case — not involving a school — a court has held on appeal that, while Rastafarians may be a religious sect, they are not an ethnic or national group (the incident involved a taxi firm refusing to employ a Rastafarian unless he agreed to cut his hair). The school could therefore insist on a reasonable haircut.

The second situation reflects the case of *Mandla v Dowel Lee* where parents insisted on their son, who was a pupil at a private school, wearing his turban because he was a Sikh. On appeal it was held that Sikhs are an ethnic group, as well as a religious one, and that to ban the turban was discriminatory. The school was ordered to readmit the pupil plus his turban.

Recent incidents in schools, which have not actually reached the courts, suggest that banning trousers for girls in mixed schools, and banning earrings for boys where girls are allowed to wear them, are both likely to be discriminatory.

52 Legal issues and the self-managing school

Avoiding discrimination

Apart from an awareness of what constitutes discrimination the following may help:

- Before an interview for staff prepare questions and check that these are not capable of being discriminatory.
- See that interviewers are aware of what may constitute discrimination.
- Record clear reasons for the final decision which are based on such factors as experience, qualifications, references and general suitability for the post — all of which clearly avoid any suggestion of discrimination.
- When constructing timetables, see that option choices are open to both boys and girls.
- See that school rules do not discriminate between the sexes unless there are good reasons for doing so, e.g. use of toilets, changing rooms and medical facilities.
- See that out-of-school activities generally are open to both boys and girls. However, single sex sports teams do not constitute discrimination though activities of a similar nature should be offered to both sexes.
- Tell staff not to divide a classroom rigidly between boys and girls for seating.
- Do not expect girls alone to carry out chores such as serving refreshments or washing up, or boys to move classroom furniture.

Discipline

An employer is entitled to take disciplinary action against employees where that is justified. Before the development of modern employment law, this was likely to be a withholding of wages or more probably instant dismissal. The employee had little course of redress. Today, good employers are expected to have a code of disciplinary procedures agreed with unions and made clear to employees on appointment. While employers are free to devise their own codes, it is normal for these to be based on models provided by the Advisory and Conciliation and Arbitration Service — ACAS. The aim is to set out clearly what is to happen if disciplinary action is taken so that both parties know their rights. Today, governors of grant-maintained schools and all others that have delegated powers of management have a responsibility to adopt such procedures with regard to teachers and

Staffing — discrimination, discipline and grievances 53

other employees. They would be wise to adopt those agreed between LEAs and the appropriate unions.

The purpose of disciplinary procedures is twofold. Their use should enable problems to be settled at grass roots level, allowing employers to take reasonable action to improve performance and conduct and prevent unfair treatment or victimisation of employees. Secondly, if any matter should reach an industrial tribunal where unfair dismissal is alleged, their use can provide evidence that the employer has given fair treatment in the form of suitable warnings to the employee. In general, the model code says that no employee should be dismissed for a first offence unless this is one of gross misconduct (see below), that each warning should give clear reasons and help or training offered to the employee to aid improvement, that union representation be allowed at each stage, that appeal against the warning be allowed and that provision be made for warnings to be struck off after a period of satisfactory conduct.

A typical set of disciplinary procedures for schools might contain the following sequence:

Informal warning

This is a clear statement that some aspect of the employee's conduct or performance is unsatisfactory and unless the matter is put right formal action will be commenced. It is given orally by the head, and no record placed on the employee's file.

Formal warning

This is the commencement of formal proceedings against the employee. The warning may be given orally but is then followed in writing and a record placed on the employee's file. It is given by the head but the chair of governors needs to be informed and the LEA if it is the employer. There may be provision for a hearing.

Final warning

This means what it says — unless substantial improvement is shown or a relatively serious matter rectified then dismissal will result. Similarly, if there is a repetition of serious misconduct then dismissal will result. Usually this will mean that previous warnings have gone unheeded. The warning may again be given orally but it will also be followed in writing and placed on the employee's file. It will be given by the person or persons designated in the procedures. In grant-maintained schools this will probably be the head. In other schools, it will probably be the head or an officer appointed by the employer.

54 Legal issues and the self-managing school

Dismissal

The employee is sacked. Each school under its agreed procedures will have its own way of dealing with the action. Governors are able to delegate decision-making powers to committees over some matters, and staffing is one of them. The head cannot take the decision to dismiss, that is a matter for governors and, since employees have a right of appeal, two groups will be needed. The first will take the decision to dismiss and the second will hear any appeal against the decision. Naturally, the governors making the first decision cannot be party to hearing the appeal. In maintained schools, the LEA as employer must carry out the dismissal so it will need to be informed and consulted at all stages before dismissal is undertaken. Failure to do so, if the governors have acted unreasonably or unfairly, could result in the school's budget being charged with any compensation payable to the dismissed employee.

Finally, it needs to be remembered that there is no requirement to go through the entire sequence listed above. Dealing with a relatively serious matter could be commenced at the formal or final stage or even result in instant dismissal without any warnings at all if gross misconduct is involved. Each matter may commence at any stage that is appropriate.

From what has been said, it can be seen that, although there is no strict requirement in law for such procedures to exist, it is highly desirable for such a code to be followed in the interests of both employer and employee.

Gross misconduct

Schools are dealing with a highly vulnerable section of the community, and society expects quite rightly that the conduct of teachers and other employees in schools should be of a high professional standard, since actions amounting to gross misconduct undermine the confidence of parents and may well place pupils at serious risk. The head and governors must take positive action in such circumstances.

What amounts to gross misconduct is not laid down by law. In schools, however, it would certainly include misconduct towards pupils of a sexual nature even if this did not amount to a criminal offence, dishonesty in the form of theft or fraud and physical abuse of pupils of a non-sexual kind. The tendency is to consider the misconduct in relation to pupils. However, it could lie in a wilful refusal to obey a reasonable instruction, it could lie in the conduct of one employee towards another. Even behaviour outside school could

Staffing — discrimination, discipline and grievances 55

qualify if the conduct was related to performance within the employment.

Suspension

This is not part of disciplinary procedures but will almost certainly be necessary where there is an allegation of serious misconduct that could lead at least to a final warning. The Articles of Government for a school will include the powers to suspend an employee. Normally the head or governors will have the power to do so whenever there is the possibility of a criminal charge in the offing, where there is a danger to pupils or the employee, or where staffing relationships might otherwise break down. The suspension must be on full pay until the matter is resolved.

What disciplinary measures might have to be considered in the following?

Incidents

A. A coloured lady teacher is subject to abuse in a staffroom by a particular colleague and is constantly referred to as a 'wog'.

B. A midday supervisor has caused considerable embarrassment to a village school by spreading rumours that the governors have no interest in its management, rarely attend meetings and positively discourage complaints by parents. As a consequence, the head is left to his own devices and it is common knowledge on the staff that he is fiddling the school funds.

C. The head has instructed the school receptionist that visitors must be treated with courtesy. There is a suspicion that this does not always happen though the head does realise the difficulties that may well exist. A letter of complaint has been received from one parent complaining that when she visited school to leave forgotten sandwiches for a child's lunch, she was told to get a grip on her daughter and give her a good smack.

D. Two boys are fighting in the playground. The teacher on duty pulls them apart but does so very roughly so that one falls onto the tarmac, scrapes his knee and has to receive simple first aid.

E. A school has a system whereby report slips are circulated to subject teachers for completion and are then passed to the form tutor for stapling into a booklet to be sent to parents. One subject teacher is always late with his reports thus holding up the process, frustrating form tutors and causing complaints from parents over the lateness.

F. A male teacher is accused of importuning in a public lavatory in a city centre but is cleared by a jury. There is no suggestion of misconduct in school.

Comments

A. The incident described here was a real one and the employer was found liable to pay compensation for the discriminatory acts of its employee. The employer could then have taken disciplinary action against the offender — and probably did so. At least a formal warning would be appropriate and possibly a final one since the behaviour had continued for some time. The lady could also have taken out a grievance procedure against her colleague.

B. There is an implied condition in each employee's contract of loyalty towards the employer. Unless the assistant can substantiate her claims against the governors and the head then disloyalty would seem to be present, though some concrete evidence of her making the comments would be necessary. A final warning or even dismissal would seem appropriate because of the damage being done to the school. Unless there is hard evidence, the remarks relating to the head are also slanderous and we shall deal with situations like this in a later chapter.

C. The reception given to visitors is always important in creating a good atmosphere. An unpleasant or hostile attitude towards parents and others can damage a school's reputation quite seriously. Heads need to impress this upon reception staff though the difficulties they face at times need to be recognised. Here there seems to be a suggestion that similar encounters may have taken place before. An informal warning at least seems to be in order.

D. Teachers are allowed to use physical force towards pupils when that is necessary for the pupil's own safety, the safety of other pupils or teachers or safety in relation to equipment or property. Indeed, not to do so might be negligent — a responsible parent would certainly separate children who were fighting and possibly injuring each other. The force must be reasonable, however, and here the teacher seems to have overstepped the mark. A formal warning would seem appropriate here with the emphasis on the excessive use of force.

E. This teacher is certainly creating ongoing problems for colleagues and the smooth functioning of the school's procedures. An informal warning could certainly be used.

F. This is difficult. The governors have to consider whether this man is a potential risk to pupils. They are entitled to decide that

Staffing — discrimination, discipline and grievances 57

he is even if there was no conviction and no evidence of misconduct in school. If so, they could dismiss — a warning would be inappropriate in this case — and face an action for unfair dismissal if necessary. Their position would be a very strong one if a conviction had resulted.

Approaching staff disciplinary problems

From what has been said, the difficulties of approaching such problems are obvious. Nevertheless they must be tackled for the maintenance of the school as an efficient organisation and as one which has the respect and support of the parents generally. The underlying approach must be one of genuine consideration for staff as individuals and the provision of support and encouragement but when, and if, that fails the taking of positive action, however unpleasant that might be.

Only the head can initiate disciplinary proceedings though pressure from governors, staff or parents may demand that these take place. These guidelines may be of help to heads:

- Ask yourself searching questions as to the standards of competence and conduct that are to be expected of all staff, teaching and otherwise.
- Where these standards are not being met, look for ways in which they may be raised. There is no need to rush into the use of disciplinary procedures.
- Investigate what may be achieved by advice, encouragement, changes in timetable or duties or training. Involve other senior staff and perhaps help from outsiders such as LEA advisers.
- Have a clear grasp of the disciplinary procedures applicable to your school.
- See that all staff are aware of the existence and significance of the procedures.
- Never commence a procedure in the heat of the moment. Think about it calmly and rationally.
- Consult others for their opinions — senior staff, chair of governors or a fellow head.
- When a warning is given, always have a witness present. See that the right to union presence is always explained, that rights of appeal are stated, and that there is provision for the removal of the warning from the employee's record after a period of satisfactory service.
- Explain exactly why the warning is being given and stress the harm that is being done to the individual's reputation and that of the school.

58 Legal issues and the self-managing school

- Explore with the employee ways in which help might be given in order to put matters right.
- Try to end with the feeling that all is not lost if only. . . .

Grievance procedure

Disciplinary procedures are used by employer against staff. Grievance procedures allow staff to make complaints against the employer or other employees.

Governors are required by law to adopt grievance procedures for their schools and will almost certainly adopt the model found in the Burgundy Book or some local variation of this which has been agreed with teacher unions and those representing other employees. A separate procedure exists for heads.

Grievance procedures are not intended to deal with situations involving a group of staff having a complaint against the head or the employer — that should be dealt with under a collective disputes agreement.

Grievance procedures usually have the following features:

- A grievance should first be referred to the employee's immediate superior. In most schools that will be the head, but in large ones it could be the head of a faculty or large department.
- An effort should be made to settle the grievance informally.
- If that fails then the grievance should be referred elsewhere — that may be to the head but will usually be to a committee of the governors with delegated powers or to the governors themselves. There may be provision for further appeals.
- Union representation should be allowed at all stages.

Case

Mrs H teaches at a primary school where the head has, as part of planned directed time, allowed for a member of staff to be on duty for 15 minutes before school commences each morning and for 15 minutes after school ends in the afternoon. Mrs H is a single parent with two young children and getting them ready for school in the morning is difficult and time-consuming. She is put on duty before school frequently and rarely after school though she had arrangements with a neighbour to collect her children from school and look after them until her return. She feels that she is being treated unfairly.

Mrs H should take her grievance to the head who may not be fully aware of her problems. She cannot complain of being given a share of supervision duties — providing these are in directed time — but she is

Staffing — discrimination, discipline and grievances 59

entitled to such duties being allocated fairly within that time. If the matter cannot be settled amicably between herself and the head — if, for example, she is told to do as she is told within directed time — then she may take her grievance to the governors who may issue an instruction to the head.

In the interests of harmony and good working relationships the settlement of grievances without recourse to formal procedures is obviously highly desirable.

Summary

When dealing with all staffing arrangements and problems, employers and their agents need to be aware of what constitutes discrimination, and take positive steps to avoid it.

School managers need to be aware of their disciplinary and grievance procedures and to apply these strictly to incidents that occur so that the rights of all concerned are observed. However, wherever possible, problems should be settled informally in the interests of good working relationships within the school. If that fails, the action taken should be clear and positive.

7 Dismissal, tribunals and remedies

A contract of service may come to an end in various ways. In most cases it will be by agreement between the parties, usually by the employee giving due notice. It may be the conclusion of a fixed-term or upon the occurrence of a pre-determined event such as the return of another employee after illness or pregnancy. It may end because of frustration, that is some event which makes performance by one or both parties impossible — some severe physical incapacity perhaps or a prison sentence or reaching the age of compulsory retirement. It may end by dismissal, and it is in such cases that serious problems may arise for school managers.

Cases

A. Darby is a laboratory technician in a secondary school. He is competent at his work in the preparation of materials and servicing of equipment but very slack over security, leaving laboratories and cupboards unlocked. He has been given informal warnings and, after complaints by the head of science, a formal warning which has been placed on his file. This records that he has been given the opportunity to attend a course on safety procedures for laboratory technicians. He has not taken up the offer.

The head receives a visit from an angry parent carrying a bottle which contains a chemical. This has been found in the pupil's satchel and he has admitted to the parent that this was taken from an unlocked cupboard in a laboratory — a cupboard for which Darby is responsible. The chemical is potentially very dangerous.

The head sends for Darby who admits leaving the cupboard unlocked and shows little remorse. There is an angry exchange and the head loses his temper. He suspends Darby forthwith and tells him that the incident will be reported to the disciplinary

continued . . .

Dismissal, tribunals and remedies   61

Cases – continued . . .

committee of the governors with a recommendation for Darby's dismissal. The committee are aware from parents of problems caused by Darby and they decide to dismiss him as they consider him a real threat to the safety of pupils. Darby now claims compensation for unfair dismissal and his job back.

B. Joan is an attractive lady teacher but rather shy and lacking a sense of humour. In the staffroom she is subjected to a great deal of comment of a sexual nature, and this develops into bottom-pinching and unwelcome close contact. She is now almost afraid to come to work. She cannot face alleging discrimination by male staff or taking out a grievance procedure and so she tenders her resignation without explaining to the head why she has done so. She now discovers that she may have a case for constructive dismissal.

Comments

A. The governors certainly have a case for disciplinary action against Darby. Under the disciplinary procedures explained in the last chapter, they might have decided that a final warning was sufficient but, since Darby has caused problems earlier, has not taken advantage of training opportunities, and has almost caused a serious accident, they have decided to bypass that stage. Perhaps they decided that his behaviour amounted to gross misconduct.

Darby could go to an industrial tribunal on the grounds that a final warning should have been given and therefore he was unfairly dismissed. Even if the tribunal accepted that, any compensation would be likely to be reduced because of his unwillingness to attend a training course and the way in which his conduct contributed to his dismissal. The governors have a strong case.

Can Darby get his job back? The tribunal may order this in the event of success by Darby but cannot force the employer to comply (see below). Darby would then gain additional compensation.

Although the governors may well succeed in this instance, both the head and the governors have caused some doubt by not giving a final warning. Perhaps this should have been given at a much earlier stage — the evidence seems to be there. Because of the hazard he has created, Darby might even be open to criminal prosecution under Health and Safety legislation.

62 Legal issues and the self-managing school

B. Joan does not appear to have been dismissed at all. Employment protection legislation, however, introduces a new concept — that of constructive dismissal. The employee may be forced to resign because of oppression, intolerable or grossly unfair treatment. Making fundamental changes in an employee's conditions of service or status may also qualify. Here, if the facts are as stated, Joan has a good case against the employer who has to take responsibility for the actions of other employees. There are a number of similar instances outside schools where compensation has been awarded.

Although the employer may be liable here, it may then take disciplinary action against the offenders.

Types of dismissal

Wrongful

In essence, this is a breach of contract, e.g. by not giving the correct amount of notice.

Unfair

When an employer broke the terms of a contract in the days before the introduction of modern employment legislation and dismissed an employee, the remedy lay in the civil courts and may still do so in theory. The cost and time involved now makes this most unlikely and, today, legislation has provided swifter and cheaper remedies. The rights involved go much further than under the terms of ordinary contracts. Almost all contracts of service are affected by the Employment Protection (Consolidation) Act 1978 and by subsequent legislation. One right given is that of seeking compensation from an industrial tribunal against the employer if a dismissal is unfair. This applies even if the employer has given correct notice. The employer must show that the dismissal was fair.

There are a number of grounds on which a dismissal may well be fair:

Capability — the employee is incapable because of ill-health, mental state or lack of necessary skills or qualifications.

Conduct — the employee refuses to obey reasonable instructions, is dishonest towards the employer, is involved in sexual misconduct in school situations, is drunk on the premises, has excessive unwarranted absence, or is involved

Dismissal, tribunals and remedies

in criminal conduct outside school which has some bearing on conduct within school.

Redundancy — work available for the employee or employees has ceased or diminished.

Other substantial reason — this is an open question but might indicate an irreconcilable clash of personalities mainly caused by the dismissed employee.

Some dismissal is automatically unfair — on grounds of pregnancy or engaging in lawful trade union activities.

As we have seen, the dismissal may have been clearly stated but it may also be construed from the conduct of the employer or of other employees which has forced the complainant to resign. It may also be construed where the employer has changed the nature of the post to such an extent that it amounts to dismissal from one post and reappointment to another.

Redundancy

This is a form of dismissal, and is likely nowadays to be a problem facing the governors of a number of schools. It needs to be approached carefully.

Case

A large county primary school is situated on a council estate where, because of little movement of population, the numbers on roll have fallen considerably. The teaching staff are stable and most are at, or near, the top of their salary scales but none is near the age for possible early retirement with benefits. In the past, the LEA has been generous over staffing but, now that the school has delegated powers, it must manage its budget. After making all possible savings the governors conclude that the only way to balance the books is to declare two members of staff redundant and so they decide to take that action.

How should their problem be approached?

1. The employer is the LEA so a check should be made to discuss what procedures have been agreed — there are certain to be some. These should be followed to the letter. They are likely to be as follows, based upon a ruling of the Employment Appeal Tribunal.

64 Legal issues and the self-managing school

2. An explanation then needs to be given to the entire teaching staff — not just those likely to be affected. This is a matter for the chair of governors and the head and should not be left to the head alone. Volunteers for redundancy should then be sought.

3. If there are volunteers, their offers may not be acceptable. Their services may be essential for the running of the school. If no suitable volunteers are forthcoming then consultation with the appropriate unions needs to take place before there is any further discussion by governors. In our case this might mean as many as four different unions and the aim of such consultation is to ensure fair treatment for all staff.

4. The possibility of redeployment needs to be investigated. The LEA as employer may suggest this to other schools with vacancies but the consent of their governors has to be obtained so redeployment is now not easy to arrange.

5. If all efforts to date have failed then a list of criteria must be drawn up and approved by the full governing body. This could range from the need to cover the teaching of all groups or specialist subjects within the school to length of service. It should not include involvement in voluntary out-of-school activities. All this may well mean the compilation of a new staffing structure. The aim should be the protection of the school's curriculum and efficient management and not that of particular individuals.

6. Our governors may well decide to give the task to a committee and could, in fact, delegate the final decision-making to it after applying the criteria. Once the decision to nominate for redundancy has been taken, those affected must be given a right of appeal against the decision and so a second group of governors — perhaps all those not on the committee — will need to hear any appeals.

If procedures similar to these are not followed then the teachers nominated for redundancy may be able to claim unfair dismissal.

Rights under redundancy

If procedures such as these have been observed then the two teachers who have been nominated will have a right to redundancy payments based upon present salary and length of service. There is a minimum laid down but many employers are more generous. The awards will have to be paid by the LEA but if our governors had acted

Dismissal, tribunals and remedies

unreasonably, for example, by not adopting reasonable criteria, the charges could be deducted from the school's budget.

In addition, the teachers made redundant must be given reasonable time off in order to seek other employment, not necessarily in teaching.

Tribunals and remedies

In Chapter 2 we explained that employment problems are dealt with by hearings known as industrial tribunals and that, though these are not strictly courts of law, they are conducted on broadly similar lines and have appeal to the Employment Appeal Tribunal, which ranks as a division of the High Court. Consequently, cases from industrial tribunals may eventually reach the House of Lords. The tribunals have a legally qualified chairman plus lay members, the hearings are conducted with a minimum of formality and legal representation is not required. It is normal for union officials to assist complainants but any other 'friend' may also do so.

The burden of proof in the first place lies with the complainant to prove that dismissal has taken place. This will be simple in most cases but difficult to justify, perhaps, where constructive dismissal is alleged. If the tribunal accepts that dismissal has indeed taken place then it lies with the employer to show that the dismissal was fair. If the tribunal concludes that it was so then the complainant gets nothing. If the tribunal concludes that the dismissal was unfair then compensation will be awarded as shown below. Either party may ask for the tribunal's reasons for decision to be put in writing.

Compensation and orders may be as follows.

Basic award

This is usually equivalent to what the employee would have received if he or she had been made redundant.

Compensatory award

This is an additional sum at the tribunal's discretion and is intended to cover aspects not included in the basic award such as loss of pension rights and loss of earnings up to the time of the hearing. An employee who has contributed to the dismissal by some form of misconduct or who has failed to make reasonable efforts to find new employment may have this award reduced accordingly.

Special award

This is an additional payment if the dismissal is on grounds of engaging in lawful union activities. It is also payable where the tribunal orders reinstatement or reengagement and the employer refuses to comply.

Reinstatement

This means that the employee should be given the same job back with the same status and conditions. The employer may argue that this is impracticable because of the impossibility of reestablishing good working relationships with colleagues or indeed in schools because of the possible animosity of pupils or parents.

Reengagement

This means that the employer should find the employee similar work in a similar establishment or area under the same conditions. Before delegation of powers to governors, this was always possible in school situations with the LEA finding a similar post in another school and there were instances of this happening. Now, unless the governors of another school agree, reengagement is impossible and so again the employer may complain that it cannot comply.

Summary

Dismissal may take place on grounds of incapability, redundancy, misconduct or some other substantial reason. Even if the dismissal is not explicit, it may be construed from the conduct of the employer or that of other employees. If a dismissed employee takes a case to an industrial tribunal then the employer must be prepared to show that the dismissal was fair. If the ruling is that it was unfair then the employee is awarded compensation but the employer cannot be forced to take the employee back or to find him or her a similar post.

8　Parental duties

A governing body is responsible to parents for the conduct of the school, and those parents have a number of rights which must be observed. Parents also have duties, and schools need to understand those duties and what can be insisted upon.

Duties of parents

The primary duty of educating a child lies with the parents, not the State. S.36 of the 1944 Act makes this clear:

> It shall be the duty of the parent of every child of compulsory school age to cause him to receive efficient full-time education suitable to his age, ability and aptitude, [and to any special educational needs he may have] either by regular attendance at school or otherwise.

Parents may therefore educate children at home themselves — an increasing number decide to do so — and, while that education should measure up to the standard laid down above, it does not have to comply with the National Curriculum. Parents, if they can afford it, may educate their children by employing private tutors and, again, this does not have to comply with the National Curriculum. They may send their children to private schools and still the National Curriculum is not obligatory. Otherwise they must send their children to a school provided by the State where the National Curriculum does apply and where the LEA has a legal obligation to see that sufficient schools are provided.

According to age, ability and aptitude

The inference is that sending a child to a state school where the National Curriculum is implemented complies with that duty.

68   Legal issues and the self-managing school

However, if it could be shown that a child required special treatment, say, because of blindness or severe deafness, and the parents refused to allow that special treatment to be given then they could certainly be in breach of their duty.

The courts have largely been silent as to what constitutes an 'efficient education' and that given to many children at home hardly seems to qualify.

Regular attendance

If a child is on the admission register then the law requires that the attendance be regular and parents have a duty to see that this is complied with. What constitutes regular attendance has been the subject of several legal cases which have, to a certain extent, clarified the law.

- A pupil who is absent, even for a single session, without a reasonable cause makes a parent commit an offence.
- The reasonable cause must be one concerning the pupil personally and not for the sake of others. Illness qualifies, the illness of others does not.
- A pupil who arrives after the class register has been closed is absent as far as the law is concerned, and so the parents commit an offence.
- There is a right to absence for two weeks in any academic year for holiday purposes, not necessarily with parents.
- It is a defence to a prosecution to show that an authorised person has granted leave of absence.
- It is also a defence that the pupil is entitled to free transport to school and that transport has not been provided.

The school's approach to problems of attendance

The law then lays a strict duty on the parents of pupils attending school. They must see that their attendance is regular. Schools have a duty to monitor attendance and to initiate action if it is unsatisfactory. The school prospectus must now record the rate of unauthorised absence that has taken place. Clearly, it is important for a close watch to be kept on attendance both for the sake of the pupil and for the good name of the school. And truancy is contagious. Once a few are absent and nothing is done then others will soon follow. Truants soon become bored and turn to drug-taking, shoplifting and other criminal

Parental duties 69

activities, and the morale of the school is soon undermined. So how should the school approach attendance?

The most obvious way to ensure good attendance is to create a situation where children want to come to school. Interesting and stimulating delivery of a curriculum and other activities suitable to the needs and capabilities of pupils is fundamental. So is an approach to pastoral care that fosters a climate of good but firm relationships between staff and pupils and the sense of community that this encourages. An essential element in this approach will be the concern of the class or group tutor for individual pupils with close attention to their attendance and an awareness of the possible reasons for absence. Free and ungrudging contact with parents themselves will be another important factor. Sometimes the reasons for absence will lie beyond the teacher's or the school's powers to help, and then legal measures will have to be taken. That should be a last resort but not subject to excessive delay when other efforts have failed.

Mary

She has just transferred from a small primary school to a large comprehensive at some distance from her home. She has to catch a bus at 8.15 and does not arrive home until 4.30 each day. She is of average ability and her primary school record indicates problems with calculations and reading but her talent at art is high. Her record of attendance at the primary school was good and she seems to come from a home where there is concern for her welfare though there are several other children and the family is on low income. The mother has given some practical help to the class teacher at the primary school.

Mary attends well for the first few weeks at the secondary school but then she begins to have absences for stomach upsets. This gets worse and soon she refuses to come to school at all. Her mother has become very anxious because of Mary's obvious unhappiness and unwillingness to attend. She finds it difficult to visit the school because she has other children to look after and she has no transport. When the welfare officer visits, she blames the school for what is happening but can give no precise complaint. She knows that Mary must attend and she is now in fear of prosecution.

This is a clear case where legal remedies are inappropriate even though technically the parents have committed an offence. The parent is willing to send Mary to school and needs help, not prosecution, or even the threat of it. Why is Mary not attending?

It may be that she cannot cope with the work in her new school. Is she in the right groups for her ability level? Perhaps some movement would help. Perhaps some extra help with calculations or reading would restore her confidence. Could her talent at art be used in some way?

70 Legal issues and the self-managing school

Has she run foul of a particular teacher or particular pupils? Perhaps she is being bullied on the bus or while waiting for it. A sensible older pupil could help. Perhaps the class tutor may be able to get some clues from other pupils. The class teacher from the primary school may have some ideas.

There needs to be close discussion between the school and the mother. She could be brought to school by the welfare officer, or the school could send someone from the staff to the home since there seems a desire to co-operate.

The real reason for her absence may be quite simple. She does not have full uniform and others laugh at her; she cannot find a seat on the bus and is being pushed around; one teacher has spoken harshly to her and she has this teacher almost every day; she is afraid of stripping off in the changing room for PE. The reason may be much more complicated and need outside help from the medical or psychology services.

Martha

She is in her fourth year at a secondary school. She is a girl of considerable intelligence but is under-achieving. She finds class work relatively easy and is clever enough just to get by. Her attendance has been sporadic, but she has never been absent for long periods and has always brought a note to explain her absence which has often been on a Monday.

Martha comes from a home that is reputedly a difficult one. Her parents have had no contacts with the school during her time there. They have not attended parents' evenings. Rumour has it that mother and father spend a great deal of time in local pubs and Martha has been known to have brought an odd can of beer into school. She is often told off because of the amount of make-up she wears and for her efforts to flout the school rules over dress. Her interest in older boys is obvious — they wait for her outside the school gates.

Her attendance has now become a great deal worse and the welfare officer has visited the home. It was dirty and neglected. He found the father and mother unco-operative, aggressive even. Their attitude is that Martha is now old enough to look after herself and the inference is that she is not going to be allowed to interfere with their pleasures. Yes, they do leave her to her own devices at night but she is expected to go to bed at ten o'clock. Her boy friends are not the school's business and, if they choose to let her stay out late at weekends, that is their affair. She has no time for teachers and the school and neither do they.

Although this is a case where legal action may well be necessary, the school seems to have been slack over dealing with Martha's attendance. The earlier sporadic absence should have given warning signals and that on Mondays suggests weekends misspent. Positive

Parental duties 71

efforts should have been made to contact the parents — her work and behaviour provided ample opportunities. The welfare officer should have visited the home earlier. The parents might have responded if earlier contact had been made. They may indeed have made limited efforts over attendance in the past.

The school now needs to make positive efforts to arouse Martha's interest in school, perhaps through a member of staff with whom she does have a good relationship, perhaps by stressing her capability of obtaining good qualifications and employment. It may not be too late to obtain the co-operation of the parents.

If these efforts fail then Martha's continued absence will be a bad example to others, an irritation to other parents who make efforts to get their children to school and believe Martha is 'getting away with it', and a message to staff that their efforts at monitoring are a waste of time.

A clear warning then needs to be given to Martha's parents followed by a prosecution if necessary. In addition, social services need to be alerted since there may be evidence of serious neglect, lack of control and perhaps something worse.

Registers

Regulations as to the keeping of registers by schools have been in force since the Pupils' Registration Regulations of 1956 and these have now been updated by the Education (Pupils' Attendance Records) Regulations of 1991.

Schools are required by law to keep registers of two types. The first is an admission register which records for each pupil the full name, sex, names and addresses of all known to have parental responsibility, date of birth, exact date of admission and name and address of last school attended. This register may now be computerised providing the school is registered under the Data Protection Act. The regulations list the circumstances under which a pupil's name may be removed from the admission register, and these include registration at another school, the parents certifying that they will educate the child at home, the pupil is known to have moved so far away that attendance at the school is not feasible, there has been absence for more than four weeks, and enquiries have failed to discover the reason, or that an attendance order naming the school has been changed.

The second type of register that must be kept is the class register. This is a legal document and that for Martha's class would have to be produced as evidence in court if her parents were to be prosecuted so its accuracy is important. Class registers must be kept for three years after the end of the academic year to which they refer.

The DFE issues a circular of guidance on the keeping of class registers. This suggests the symbols that might be used but whether the school uses these or not the register must be marked at the commencement of each session and it must indicate presence or absence. The absence must indicate whether it was authorised or unauthorised. Late arrival must also be clearly recorded.

The school will need to have some procedure for checking absences in order to identify possible problems at an early stage and this procedure needs to be made clear to parents, perhaps in the school prospectus. If a pupil is absent then an explanation could be asked for by telephone or letter as soon as possible. Any absence lasting for three days or more without reasonable explanation could be the subject of a written request by first-class post to the parent asking for the reason. If no response was received then the welfare officer could be asked to visit. The welfare officer could also be asked to investigate patterns of absence, e.g. Mondays in Martha's case. A system on these lines should enable most absences to be dealt with before they get out of hand.

School rules

Do parents have a duty to see that their children obey school rules? Statute is silent but there are two grounds for saying that they have such a duty.

The first comes from decided cases in the courts. In one instance the judge commented, ' . . . the law requires of parents of children who attend . . . schools . . . a reasonable co-operation'. This case concerned a pupil refusing to obey instructions. Other cases have stressed that providing rules are reasonable they must be followed and parents can be expected to exercise control over their children in following them. Martha's parents are hardly fulfilling their duty in this respect.

The second comes from the fact that children do not have to attend school — they may be educated otherwise. Parents now have a wide choice of schools and, if they are unhappy over the rules of a school, they may choose another. If the rules are made clear before the parents make their choice then it is reasonable for them to accept those rules and support the school's reasonable application of them.

Parental duties

73

Care and control

Certainly parents are responsible for the welfare and upbringing of their children, at least until the age of 16, and they may be prosecuted for neglecting or abusing them and, of course, the children may be removed from them if they are at serious risk or badly neglected. In some circumstances, parents may be punished for criminal offences committed by their children, and there are moves to widen such powers. Since Mrs Gillick's case and the provisions of the Children Act 1989, this does not mean that children do not have the right to a voice over decisions affecting them but the basic responsibility lies with the parents.

Other duties?

There are some other areas where schools might like to see duties laid upon parents but the law has not done so. There is no duty for parents to explain the reason for a pupil's absence — the authorities must take action if they suspect a breach of the law. There is no duty to respond to letters from school, to attend parents' evenings, or to consult with the school in any way. There is no duty to see that pupils wear uniform, only that they are clean and reasonably dressed. There is no duty to help or co-operate at home with school work, and there is no duty to provide books and equipment.

Summary

Parents have a legal duty to see that their children are well cared for. They must see that they are educated and if they attend school their attendance must be regular. The school may expect reasonable support from them over discipline and over the application of school rules.

9 Parental rights

The Swifts

Mr and Mrs Swift are a young married couple whose oldest child, Dean, will soon be starting school for the first time. They have the impression that, since their day, there have been great changes in schools which now, according to what they have read and seen on television, have become more accountable to parents. The spate of legislation passed during the last few years has apparently not only allowed schools to manage their own affairs but has ensured that parents are treated almost as customers for educational services. Parents have a say in what happens in decision-making in schools, they are able to know what is going on in what used to be almost closed communities. They have rights which have to be observed.

Mr and Mrs Swift will send Dean to a state school and would like to choose the one for him to attend. They expect to discover details of that school, its curriculum and how it is run. Once Dean has begun his education there they want to know how he is getting on, to visit the school and talk to his teachers about his progress. If it turns out that he has special problems they hope that these will be catered for. They believe that children need to be aware of moral issues, should have an understanding of religious beliefs and be encouraged to take a wide interest in cultural and sporting activities. They realise that parental support for a school is important, and they would be prepared to become involved with school activities if opportunities occurred.

Most of the expectations of Mr and Mrs Swift can now be defined as rights rather than hopes and those which schools are under a legal duty to observe. Some may not be quite as definite as they imagine.

Choice of school

This is a case in point. The concept of a free choice of school is not really new because the 1944 Act stated that children were to be educated according to the wishes of their parents. However, those

Parental rights 75

endeavouring to exercise choice of school came up against the fact that each school had its own defined catchment area, and to obtain a place at a school outside that area was very difficult indeed. Legislation since 1944 has always given the impression that parents have a choice of school but it has been restricted by statements that it must not incur unreasonable public expenditure or inefficient use of resources. Yet there is now some greater freedom of choice.

Freedom of choice of school has been increased by two factors: the abolition of strict catchment areas and falling rolls which have created surplus places in many schools. In theory, Mr and Mrs Swift may visit any schools they wish and then decide which one Dean will attend. The school they choose may be just outside what is considered to be their normal area and it may be full, i.e. up to its standard number. They will not be able to claim a place for Dean. They may not like the local schools and may find one ideally suited to their ideas but situated some miles away. There is a place but no transport is available and they are unable to take Dean to school each day and collect him. In practice, some parents have free choice, others do not.

Each school must have an agreed admissions policy and a standard number. Both must be published as part of the information for parents. Responsibility for doing this lies with the LEA or the governors of aided, special agreement or grant-maintained schools. Arrangements for the calculation of the standard number for primary schools will be found in the Education (Variation of Standard Numbers for Primary Schools) Order 1991; an important factor is physical capacity. For secondary schools, the number is based on the number of pupils admitted in 1979, except for new schools opened since that time. There are DFE circulars which give advice and complicated arrangements for schools which wish to have their standard numbers changed.

Information

If the right to choose a school is hedged about with some doubts the right to information for parents is not. This right is probably the greatest change that has come about with the passing of recent legislation.

In Chapter 4 we saw that parents are entitled to an annual report from the governing body indicating how it has been discharging its duties for the overall management of the school during the previous year. There must also be a school prospectus.

As yet there has been no definition of 'prospectus' but the information the document must contain is such that a simple letter will not do. The prospectus must include: the school's name, address

76 Legal issues and the self-managing school

and telephone number; the names of the head and the chair of governors; the type of school and any religious affiliation or foundation; the structure for teaching purposes; the policy over homework; arrangements for pupil discipline, pastoral care and children with special educational needs; policy over school uniform; policy over charging and remissions; the timings of the school day; details of the rate of unauthorised absence; and the most recent examination results for pupils in years 11 and 13.

As far as the curriculum is concerned, the prospectus must give a summary of the written statement on the curriculum which the school has given to the LEA. It must list the external qualifications that may be taken at the school and the relevant syllabuses that apply. It must explain the LEA's arrangements for hearing complaints about the curriculum, and it must indicate how parents may inspect or obtain certain documents relating to the curriculum as implemented in the school.

Those documents include: schemes and syllabuses of work, the prospectus, the annual report to parents, any official reports by inspectors and copies of DFE circulars and relevant statutory instruments.

Parents are also entitled to an annual report on a pupil's educational achievements, including National Curriculum subjects and examination results plus details of other subjects studied and activities undertaken.

How to comply with the law

- Spend a considerable effort on the prospectus. Schedule 2 of the Education (Schools Information) Regulations 1981 gives the main requirements, with items related to the curriculum, school times and unauthorised absence added later. Include other items which will be useful for projecting the image of the school with photographs and art work if that is possible. Ensure that the standard of reproduction is high and that the language used is as simple as possible and avoids jargon.
- Consider including school rules in the prospectus. This could be useful in the case of future arguments but remember that unreasonable or unworkable rules so quoted could be used against you.
- Have a collection of documents most likely to be asked for by parents available in the school front office. Mention this in the prospectus, on newsletters to parents, and at parents' meetings.

Parental rights 77

- Check the format and likely content of reports to parents, and see that these meet the legal requirements.
- Consider individual pupil records of achievement since these will supply much of the extra material that is required and is desirable.
- Make sure that the prospectus is thoroughly revised annually to take account of changes in the law and in the school's own circumstances.

Curriculum

This is another area where parental rights are limited. If Mr and Mrs Smith send Dean to a state school then they have little choice but to accept the curriculum of that school. It must, of course, comply with the National Curriculum and parents have a legal entitlement to that, but whatever additional elements are provided is a matter for the school. Parents have a right to know the content of the curriculum but they cannot directly influence how it is delivered in the classrooms. That is a professional matter for the head and staff.

One element over which parents have some influence, through the governing body, is the question of sex eduation. Whether this should form part of the curriculum or not is a matter for the governing body to decide. If sex education is to be part of the curriculum then it must have due regard to morals and family life, and it is compulsory for all pupils unless the governors allow parents the right of withdrawal.

The one aspect where parents have a clear right of withdrawal is that of religious education and worship. County schools have to follow a syllabus of religious education agreed by the local SACRE (Standing Advisory Council for Religious Education). Voluntary schools usually follow this also but may vary it at the request of parents in accordance with its deed of trust. Aided schools devise their own syllabuses according to their trust deed and religious affiliation. Grant-maintained schools use the syllabus which was agreed and in use before their change of status.

Schools must hold a corporate act of worship each day which, unless excusal has been given by the SACRE, must, on most occasions, be mainly or wholly Christian in tone. The assembly does not have to be of the entire school, there may be a number of small ones, and it does not have to be at the beginning of the day. Parents have a right to withdraw their children from acts of worship but not from any other assemblies which may be held.

Earlier we said that parents have a right for the National Curriculum to be provided. Does this mean that it must be provided in its entirety for all pupils, whatever their individual capabilities?

78 Legal issues and the self-managing school

The answer is no. The head is able to excuse a pupil temporarily from elements of the National Curriculum where that appears to be in the pupil's best interests. The position must be reviewed every six months, and parents have a right of appeal against such excusals. Excusal for a longer term may take place where a pupil is the subject of a statement of special educational needs.

Special educational needs

Let us suppose that, after he has been attending school for some time, it becomes clear that Dean is having problems with reading and that Mr and Mrs Swift are becoming anxious over this. They believe that he needs special help.

The Education Act 1981 gives them rights in such a matter. They can request that the LEA make an assessment of Dean — the initiative could have come from the LEA at the prompting of the school. The LEA must comply unless the request is completely unreasonable. If the result indicates that Dean has a learning difficulty well beyond that of most children of his age then the LEA may make a 'statement' of those needs and how it intends to provide for them. It may decide that no statement is necessary. This does not mean that Dean has no needs but that they must be provided for within the normal conduct of the school. In other words, no special help will be provided from outside.

Unless Dean's reading difficulties are really severe, it is unlikely that a statement will be made in his case. Mr and Mrs Swift have the right of appeal to a panel set up by the LEA, to the Secretary of State or even to seek judicial review from the courts.

Other rights

We have spent some time in examining the rights of parents over admission of pupils to schools, the information that must be made available to them, the position over the curriculum and the provision for special educational needs because these are aspects most likely to create problems for schools.

There are other rights and some of these have been suggested in earlier chapters. The additional rights for Mr and Mrs Swift can be summarised thus:

- The right to stand for election as parent governors and the right to stand as candidates in such an election.
- The right to receive an annual report from the governors and attend an annual meeting for parents to discuss this report.

Parental rights   79

- The right, with other parents, to initiate a ballot for an application for grant-maintained status and to vote in such a ballot.
- The right to a report on Dean's performance at school and consultation with staff about this.
- The right to make complaints to the governing body or to the LEA on a number of matters.
- The right to appeal against decisions relating to admission or exclusion of a pupil or to excusal from aspects of the National Curriculum.
- The right to expect that teachers will comply with their conditions of service and will behave towards pupils as responsible parents would do.
- The right to visit the school for legitimate purposes.
- The right to expect the school to comply with health and safety legislation.

These last three items will be dealt with in greater detail in later chapters.

Parent–teacher associations

Although there have been suggestions that some form of home–school association should be required by law, at present there is no such requirement. If this should take place in the future then it would raise questions of the legal standing of the group, its constitution, powers and responsibility for finance and other matters.

The present position is that a school does not have to have any form of PTA. If one is formed by parents then the governors may even refuse to allow it to meet on school premises or even to acknowledge its existence. The group is what is known in law as an unincorporated association, it is similar to an amateur sports club, a dramatic society or a gardening club. It makes its own constitution, makes its own rules, elects its own officers and is responsible for its own finance. Its officers may sue on behalf of the association and may themselves be sued. The school governors have no responsibility for its affairs though its insurance over the use of school premises would have to be monitored carefully.

Tactless though it might be, the governors could charge the PTA for the use of the premises. They could also ban the association from holding events likely to cause problems over consumption of alcohol or which presented risks of fire.

Not all schools are willing to have PTAs. During 26 years as a head of secondary schools, the writer had experience of dealing with many

PTAs. The result was almost always very much to the good of the school in terms of fostering relationships, aiding communication and raising finance. It was necessary, however, for the head and other staff to become involved and, as tactfully as possible, have an influence on the activities decided upon. Perhaps the best approach is to encourage the PTA to join the National Confederation of Parent Teacher Associations which offers a magazine, advice, conferences and some financial benefits over insurance. Its model constitution is a sound one for any PTA.

Summary

Parents do not have the right to dictate how pupils shall be taught. They do have many other rights, as outlined here, which schools need to acknowledge and observe.

10 Pastoral care and discipline

In this chapter, and the next, we explore problems relating to pupils which may well have legal implications. Since pupils are the reason for the school's very existence the handling of such problems is vital to the well-being and efficiency of that school, its image in the eyes of parents and the local community and the development of young people into responsible individuals who will play a full part in adult life.

Pastoral care

The term itself is vague and means different things to different people in different contexts. In a few secondary schools it is used largely to define a system, such as house or year groupings, which exists mainly for administrative purposes and little else. At the other end of the spectrum, it may describe an approach heavily weighted towards probing into each individual's concerns, family background and family circumstances with little concern for any overall structure for the school as a community. Most schools fall somewhere between these two extremes.

Schools have a responsibility to see that pupils benefit as much as possible from their education. This will happen only if children are confident and adjusted to school life, interested in their work and in other school activities, making satisfactory progress and enjoying good relationships with staff and fellow pupils. A number of internal factors may militate against this, bullying and difficulties over work are good examples. There may well be external factors which cause similar barriers: unhappiness at home, ill-treatment or abuse by parents or others, drug-taking or other criminal activities, and these may well be beyond the power of the school to deal with.

82 Legal issues and the self-managing school

Each school therefore needs to devise a policy for pastoral care. In a small primary school this may not need a structured system as such but it does need agreed aims, a concerted approach and an agreement as to monitoring and action to be taken. In larger schools, a structured approach will be needed to ensure that policies are carried out and action taken.

Jan

He is eight years old and attends a very small primary school where there are only two teachers. He lives in an isolated moorland cottage where conditions are bordering on the primitive. Father and mother are casual farm workers and raise a few animals themselves. They are both semi-literate and seem to believe that, as long as Jan learns the basics of reading, writing and simple arithmetic, that will do. At times they keep him off school to help at home but hardly often enough to warrant prosecution. Jan is usually reasonably clean but is often very badly dressed. He often appears tired — he has to walk almost a mile to school — and is only making very slow progress with his schoolwork. He shows a keen interest in lessons dealing with nature and animals but in very little else.

There is a suspicion that, when he transfers to the distant secondary school, his attendance will deteriorate even further. A considerable walk will be involved in order to catch the bus.

There is no need for a complicated structure here but the governors and the head are responsible for seeing that there is a policy which will have a concern for Jan's welfare and will take action to deal with the problems that are clearly present. This could include:

- An awareness by Jan's teacher of his background and lack of progress. This could hardly go unnoticed here.
- Efforts by staff to discuss his lack of progress and stress the need for better attendance. If these fail then alert the welfare officer to visit the home again and assess conditions there.
- Explore the reasons for Jan's tiredness. As a country boy this is unlikely to be the walk to school. There may be some medical condition or poor diet. Early morning work at home perhaps.
- Try to arouse his interest in schoolwork through his knowledge of nature and animals. He may well be able to demonstrate this to other pupils and this should be a boost to his confidence.
- If the school suspects that Jan is being neglected at home and this is confirmed by the welfare officer then an early contact needs to be made with social services. The poor attendance opens the door to some tactful investigation. Some legal action may then be needed.

Pastoral care and discipline 83

- If the problems continue then see that the secondary school is alerted well before Jan's transfer.

If Jan's problems are tackled early, his attendance improved, the co-operation of his parents obtained, and progress made in his work, then all could be well. If not, then the situation will almost certainly become a great deal worse with the additional strain that secondary transfer will undoubtedly bring.

Sally

She is aged 14 and attends an inner-city comprehensive school which operates a year system of pastoral care. She is of good average ability and, until recently, has seemed to be performing up to her potential and there have been no problems over attendance and behaviour. There has always been a limited response from parents to school communications and mother has attended some parents' evenings.

Her latest report indicates a serious decline in her standards of work and she has been in some minor trouble with several teachers over defiance in class. Other girls in the class resent what they consider to be her arrogant attitude and there is a suspicion that she is being subjected to some verbal bullying in the playground and corridors. Mother has now visited the school and is very worried. It appears that the father left her some time ago and she now has another man living with her. Sally, from causing no trouble at home, now swears openly, has violent outbursts of temper, goes out with older boys and steals money and make-up from her mother. There is a suspicion of drug-taking.

In this case there needs to be a system of pastoral care which can attempt to help with at least some of Sally's problems in line with the school's policies. It is all too easy in a large school for an individual like Sally to be ignored until the problems she raises become acute, when it may well be too late. The monitoring of pastoral care, if carried out adequately, should alert the school to what is happening. The following might help:

- Within the year system there should be a form tutor who knows Sally well and will have some idea of what is happening. That teacher, in consultation with the senior colleague responsible for the year group, should be encouraged to explore Sally's difficulties.
- If those difficulties lie in school because of her work — often the cause — then help and advice can be given. If bullying is the problem then that can be tackled at source.
- If, as seems likely, the problems originate at home then the form tutor and senior staff need to have contact with mother so that she is aware of what is happening in school and how this may be a reflection of outside conditions.

84 Legal issues and the self-managing school

- Sally is growing up. It is natural for her to want boy-friends, make-up and pocket money. A certain amount of rebellion is only to be expected. Is the mother being too restrictive? Perhaps there is resentment at the new man in her mother's life since he has affected what has been a good relationship.
- The mother seems genuinely concerned. Through personal contact, the staff need to work in co-operation with her to decide how best to proceed. This needs to be done carefully since Sally's response may be the assumption that both school and mother are ranged against her.
- Other staff may be able to help — she may have a particularly good relationship with a subject teacher. Other pupils may be able to help — that could certainly be so over the bullying.
- If early solutions cannot be found then it may be necessary to involve outside agencies, the educational psychologist perhaps, the family doctor or social services. The last should certainly be involved if there is any truth in the drug-taking.

It is important that the contact with Sally is close and personal, and that can best be done by the form tutor who, in almost all cases, should be the fundamental unit in any pastoral care system. But the system should see that the form tutor is not left alone and has nominated senior staff to whom reference can be made, who will give support and guidance and who has responsibility to become involved if needed.

If Sally's problems cannot be solved easily by the form tutor and the senior member responsible for the entire year group then they must not be allowed to escalate without an awareness going through the system right to the head so that all possible action may be taken.

In the end, the school's efforts may be in vain — what is happening outside has too strong an influence — but the school must be able to say that it has done its best to discharge its responsibilities towards Sally and her mother.

Bullying

The most difficult internal task involving pastoral care is likely to be that of combating bullying. It happens in all schools, and any head who believes that it does not occur in his or her school is not facing up to reality. It is not confined to schools — it happens in the workplace and in other group situations though its methods may have considerable subtlety about them.

Children in school situations are notoriously prone to bully and be bullied and it is often the case that those who have suffered most from

Pastoral care and discipline 85

bullying become the worst bullies themselves — bullying becomes part of the subculture that exists in all schools. It can have very serious consequences and there have been a number of suicides where bullying at school seems to have been the root cause.

Bullying and the fear of it prevents any pupil from working properly and maintaining good relationships. It may be of a physical or verbal kind — the latter being the most difficult to deal with. Any pastoral care policy needs to address the problem.

- The basic approach is to acknowledge that bullying exists and to ensure that all staff are on the alert for signs of it. That includes support staff who often see pupils in informal situations where bullying is easier than under the eye of a teacher.
- There needs to be an awareness that, while those who are being bullied need help, so do the bullies. They need to be made aware of the harm they are doing to themselves as well as to others.
- Staff on supervision need to pay close attention to areas where bullying is most likely to take place: playgrounds, corridors, toilets, obscure corners of the premises.
- Signs of physical bullying will usually be obvious but those of the oral kind may be much more difficult to spot and deal with since there may be no positive evidence other than the complaints of the victim.
- Pupils need to be involved in frank discussions on bullying and its prevention. Pupil courts dealing with incidents of bullying have been successful in some schools.
- The greatest fear among primary school pupils over transfer to secondary schools is that of bullying and 'initiation' practices such as ducking or bumping. Firm action needs to be taken to stop them.
- A climate of trust and confidence in staff should enable those who are being bullied to go to teachers without hesitation. Staff need to work hard to create that climate.

External agencies

The approach to pastoral care by any school will need to include an awareness of the necessity at times to contact outside agencies. This is not usually because of what is happening inside school but because of external events which the school can do little about. There is no legal duty on schools to investigate the activities of pupils outside schools when they are the responsibility of parents or the conditions under

86   Legal issues and the self-managing school

which they live but there is certainly a moral and professional duty to alert agencies when serious problems seem to exist. Teachers are better placed than most to recognise the symptoms of those problems.

Sally again

Sally's behaviour in school has improved somewhat and the bullying seems to have subsided — perhaps another victim has been found. She is now doing well enough at her work to satisfy her teachers, though this may be an intelligent effort to prevent further intrusion into her private life.

Then the school receives this anonymous letter:

Dear head,

You don't know me but I live near Sally ————. I can tell you that girl is trouble. I've seen her smoking what they call pot with her mates near here. And I've seen her nicking things from the supermarket but nobody seems to care. And the man who lives with her mother hits them both, you can hear them screaming. Probably he has it off with both I shouldn't wonder but Mrs ———— is afraid to say anything.

Somebody should do something. Why don't you?

Yours

Normally, it is best to ignore anonymous letters, which are often motivated by spite but this one does make serious allegations concerning a girl who has previously created problems. It warrants contact with outside agencies. The obvious one here is social services. They are responsible for child protection measures and have to keep a register of those who are at risk. The school should be aware of pupils who are on it. Presumably Sally is not.

The school should have a senior member of staff nominated to co-ordinate the workings of the pastoral care system and to make contact with outside agencies. Since there are allegations of criminal offences here relating to physical abuse, sexual offences against a girl under 16 and drugs, not only should services be contacted but also the police. Staff should then be on the alert for any indication of the harm that Sally may be suffering. If, after an investigation by social services, Sally is placed on the at-risk register then the school should be informed and represented at any case conferences that take place.

Children can best be protected by all agencies working together and that includes schools. The Home Office, DHSS and the DFE have jointly produced guidance on this in *Working Together: A guide to arrangements for inter-agency co-operation for the protection of children from abuse* published in 1991.

Discipline

Discipline in any school is a part of pastoral care. That is, it must help to create and maintain a well-ordered community in which individuals may develop their own talents with confidence and yet respect the needs of others and those of the school in general. The aim must be to have a framework which is as clear as possible to pupils, staff and parents, which is not overregimented and yet not too lax. It must seek to promote self-discipline as well as to assert authority. The balance is not always easy to strike.

There is a clear legal responsibility placed upon the governing body, and through it the head, to maintain discipline by setting standards of behaviour and by seeing that those standards are maintained. If discipline breaks down, the LEA may take over the running of its schools, and the DFE may take over the running of those that are grant-maintained.

Here is a typical extract from one school's Articles of Government which illustrates the position:

Discipline

8–1 It is the duty of the head:

(a) to determine measures (which may include the making of rules and provision for enforcing them) to be taken with a view to:

    (i) promoting, among pupils at the school, self-discipline and proper regard for authority;

    (ii) encouraging good behaviour on the part of those pupils;

    (iii) securing that the standard of behaviour of those pupils is acceptable; and

    (iv) otherwise regulating the conduct of those pupils;

(b) in determining any such measures:

    (i) to act in accordance with any written statement of general principles provided for him or her by the Governing Body; and

    (ii) to have regard to any guidance that they may offer in relation to particular matters; and

(c) to make any such measures generally known within the school.

8–2 The standard of behaviour which is to be regarded as acceptable at the school shall be determined by the head so far as it is not determined by the Governing Body.

8–3 The power to exclude a pupil from the school shall be exercisable only by the head.

---

88   Legal issues and the self-managing school

The governors then make a statement of general policy over discipline. They may also give specific instructions, for example, they might ban the use of a particular sanction or they might instruct the head that parents should be informed and consulted if a certain stage of disciplinary action is reached. Otherwise, the head has to set the standards of behaviour and see that these are maintained. That implies the making of rules.

School rules

There are difficulties here. To what extent should the rules be written down? Who should make them? To whom should they be communicated and by what means? Are they legally binding on both pupils and parents? What is the head's position and that of the staff if they are broken?

It is easy to believe that any members of a community are aware of rules that prevail, through what employment law might term custom and practice, even though they are not written down. That is all very well when things are going smoothly but when confrontations occur, or when accidents happen, the position can become difficult. It is always useful in a school to have rules written down to some extent and made clear to those affected by them. They need to be drafted very carefully because it is impossible to cover every eventuality, so a mere list of prohibitions will not do. Also, such a list will do little to promote self-discipline, which should be an aim of any pastoral care policy, and will provide a challenge to bolder spirits to find ways of avoiding them.

Here are the rules for one secondary school, adapted slightly, which are written down, posted in each classroom, read to pupils at the beginning of each term and recorded prominently in the staff handbook and the prospectus for parents. They were drawn up by the head in consultation with teaching and support staff, the school council for pupils, the committee of the PTA and the governors. The final version was approved by the full governing body.

School rules

General
At all times in school, and on the way to and from school and on school visits, you are expected to behave responsibly and well.

Dress

You must come to school clean and tidily dressed. The list of correct school uniform is attached.   *continued . . .*

Pastoral care and discipline

School rules – continued . . .

Arrival and departure

(i) You must be punctual. Morning school starts at 8.55 a.m. Staff will be on duty from 8.40 onwards so you should not arrive before that time since there may be no-one to take responsibility for you.

Afternoon school starts at 1.15 p.m. If you go home for lunch, you may return at any time before that since midday supervisors will be on duty.

(ii) Once you have arrived on the premises you must not leave school again without permission from your year tutor, a deputy head, or the head. An exception is at the end of morning school if you are going home to lunch. Another is for pupils in Year 11 who may leave the premises at lunchtime if they have a pass. Pupils in Years 12 and 13 may leave the premises at lunchtime without a pass.

(iii) If you have been given permission to leave the premises at times other than lunchtimes then you must sign out at the school office and sign in on your return. If you arrive at school after the registration period then you must sign in at the school office.

Safety and security

(i) You must not interfere with electrical or fire appliances, apparatus in laboratories, workshops, the computer centre, sports hall or other classrooms. If you think that any item of equipment is in bad condition and likely to be dangerous, you should tell a teacher.

(ii) You must not bring to school: knives, matches, cigarettes, radios or cassette recorders. Valuables should not be brought to school and only cash which is absolutely essential. The school cannot be responsible for valuables brought to school. For reasons of safety and security, jewellery should not be worn.

(iii) You must enter and leave the school by the side gate, not by the main entrance.

(iv) Cycling in the school grounds is forbidden for the safety of everyone. You may only bring a cycle, motorcycle or car to school by direct permission from Mr. . . . . . .

Out of bounds

(i) The front of school: delivery lorries arrive here.

(ii) Areas around and behind all mobile classrooms, the greenhouse and the sports hall.

(iii) Grass banks and verges except those surrounding the play-grounds.

(iv) The area where staff cars are parked.

(v) The locker areas during lesson time unless a teacher has given permission.

(vi) The inside of the school during breaks and lunchtimes unless the weather is wet in which case the two main halls may be used.

(vii) The churchyard at lunchtimes for those allowed off the premises.

It is easy to criticise any set of rules but these do seem to meet criteria that might be used to assess suitability.

- Each rule should be necessary, and that necessity should be obvious or at least justified. Here the reason for the front of school being out of bounds — delivery lorries calling — is spelt out. Otherwise, it might seem an arbitrary decision.
- The rules must be capable of enforcement. The areas around school buildings will have to be patrolled during all breaks and the churchyard visited at lunchtime.
- The rules should be seen to contribute to safety. Here there are direct references to dangers to be avoided — meeting traffic at the main gate, meddling with equipment, etc. Pupils themselves are encouraged to contribute positively to safety.
- The reasons for placing areas out of bounds should be easy to understand. Perhaps here there has been theft or vandalism in locker areas during lesson times. The risk of valuables or cash being lost or stolen comes over, and the school's right not to accept responsibility.
- Parents and pupils should be given clear guidance on school times and when supervision can be expected or not provided. This is done here.
- Parents and pupils also need to know how to leave the premises during session times for legitimate reasons. If pupils have to do so then here there is a clear check made. This could be vital in case of fire and useful where truancy is suspected.
- Particular trouble spots need to be dealt with. Here we have those of scattered buildings and the local churchyard — a retreat for smokers no doubt and offensive to neighbours.
- The rules should not be all prohibitions. There are attempts here to be positive. The general rule is an encouraging one for the use of common-sense. It allows the head to decide on any matter not covered specifically by the rules. It could also be dangerous. A heavy-handed overzealous approach could find almost any minor indiscretion a breach of the rules.
- The rules need to be brief and expressed in simple language. These seem to meet that requirement, could easily be displayed in classrooms and would not take long to read to pupils.
- Rules need to have a consensus of approval by those affected by them. Pupils, staff, parents and governors have been consulted here.
- Rules need to be communicated once the governors have given formal approval. That should include all prospective pupils and parents. It should include all who work in the school whether full-time, part-time or temporary.

Pastoral care and discipline   91

- The rules need to be reviewed annually or when some event occurs which reveals a serious loophole or unforeseen danger.

Dress

The rules given above mention dress and cleanliness, and provide a uniform list, but there is no statement that uniform must be worn. This is because, as the law stands, pupils in state schools cannot be compelled to wear it. Pupils in independent schools may be required to do so, unless this would be discriminatory, because that could be a term of the contract that exists between school and parents. No legally binding contract exists between parents and state schools. The question of compulsory uniform under the new powers given to governors has not been tested in the courts. A governing body which approved such a rule might provide an interesting test case.

Heads and governors may ban unsuitable clothing and may certainly take action where pupils are unclean.

Legal force

It remains to ask how far school rules have legal force. The governors have legal powers and responsibilities enshrined in their Instrument and Articles of Government. These give governors power to make decisions over discipline and delegate powers to the head. Thus, unless rules are contrary to other aspects of law such as discrimination or that concerning exclusion, or to any decisions of the governors themselves, they are binding upon pupils, parents and staff. In these days of open enrolment any parent who does not approve of the rules of a school, or some aspect of them, is free to transfer a child to another school that has a place available. Of course, the parent could always complain to the governors and ask for a change in the rules and the governors might agree. If a rule has turned out to be unworkable or unreasonable in practice, that may well be a wise course.

Case law also supports the legality of school rules and judges have stated, on more than one occasion, that the obvious person to make the rules is the head and that schools may expect reasonable co-operation from parents in seeing that those rules are observed.

Sanctions

Schools need to have considered the action to be taken against those who misbehave and are in breach of rules, and such sanctions need to

92 Legal issues and the self-managing school

be reasonable, consistently applied and understood by all. So, locking pupils in a dark cupboard, causing them to wash their mouths out with soap, tying them to chairs or ordering them to move piles of bricks from one side of the playground to the other are clearly out. Each school will have its own reasonable policies over extra work, deduction of merit marks, placing on report, and the stages at which senior staff and parents become involved. There are two, however, that need a special mention.

Detention

To the best of the writer's knowledge, there is only one case dealing with detention and that was at a county court so it did not create a binding precedent. The decision was that detaining a pupil for a short time after school as a punishment was not unlawful.

Detention is a form of trespass to the person known as false imprisonment — unlawfully restricting an individual's right of free movement. Parents have the defence of parental authority to any such action, and teachers have a similar defence as parent substitutes during normal school sessions. Detention after school may be different. Here, *in loco parentis* has ended and a parent who claims the release of his child at the normal time cannot be refused. His authority is superior to that of the school's. If detention is a recognised punishment, and the parent refuses to co-operate then the school would have to take some other action, possibly exclusion.

A further problem is that, if a pupil is detained after school as a punishment, the teacher is responsible for supervision. If the pupil is injured on the way home, there is the possibility of an action for negligence, so detention of young pupils is very risky indeed. If the pupil is entitled to free transport, and detention means missing the bus, there is still the duty to provide free transport.

All in all, detention after school hardly seems worthwhile as a sanction. If it is used then a clear warning should be given to parents. Detention during school breaks is always permissible.

Exclusion

This is the final sanction open to a school and it is the most difficult to handle since there are legal requirements which are to be found in Ss 22–27 of the Education (No. 2) Act 1986. It should be a last resort used when the behaviour of a pupil is so disruptive that good order and the learning of others is severely impaired or when there is a real threat to the safety of staff or other pupils. There is evidence that the

Pastoral care and discipline 93

number of exclusions is rising rapidly and this may well lead to further statutory control by central government.

Excluded pupils are still entitled to have education provided so, if excluded from one school, they are entitled to a place at another which has vacancies and so the process can develop into exclusion from a succession of schools. When the supply of schools has been exhausted, only the unsatisfactory recourse of home tuition remains.

Exclusion may take various forms and may vary somewhat according to the terms in the school's own Articles of Government. The following generally apply to county and controlled schools.

Up to five days in a term

The parents must be informed without delay of the reasons and the chair of governors must also be told. If the exclusion means that the pupil will miss a public examination then the LEA must be informed. Parents must be made aware of their rights.

Any other fixed period

The same rules apply but both the chair of governors and the LEA must be informed of the details and when the exclusion is to end. There will be a right of appeal. Those hearing the appeal may order immediate reinstatement.

Indefinite

The same rules apply over the giving of information and rights of appeal. Those hearing the appeal may order reinstatement or uphold the exclusion. If the LEA should order reinstatement then the head may make the exclusion permanent.

Permanent

Again, the same rules apply over information and appeals. If the governors hear the appeal and order reinstatement then the head must comply. If the LEA hears the appeal, and the decision is at odds with the wishes of the governors, then the issue is referred to an independent appeals panel which has the last word.

Important points to note:

- Exclusion procedures for individual schools are to be found in the Articles of Government.
- Only the head or acting head may exclude. For indefinite and permanent exclusions the head cannot decide to readmit.

- At all stages, parents, or pupils themselves if they are 18 or over, must be informed of the reasons for exclusion and their rights of appeal.
- The head must always comply with the directions of the governors.
- Grant-maintained, voluntary aided and special agreement schools must set up their own appeal panels. The LEA and the final appeal panel are not involved.
- Remember that, where the governors have an appeals procedure, those deciding on the appeal must not have been involved in the first hearing. If this happens it will invalidate the decision. The head should always withdraw while the decision is being reached.

Approaching exclusion appeal hearings

The head needs to study the procedures laid down in the Articles of Government and see that these are carried out to the letter since they are legal requirements.

Governors will need to be convinced that there is good cause for exclusion, and they have to balance the welfare of the school and its pupils against fair treatment for an individual and his or her parents. When approaching a hearing then the head should be able to provide:

- Details of the grounds for exclusion — records of misconduct, serious incidents and earlier measures taken to deal with the problems. This evidence needs to have been carefully logged.
- Records of correspondence to parents explaining the nature of the complaints and seeking their co-operation, together with records of meetings, or offers of meetings, and the results. The record of a letter stating that, unless matters were put right, then exclusion would follow.
- Oral testimony of witnesses to serious incidents or the testimony of senior staff who have been closely involved with the pupil's misbehaviour.

The procedures over exclusion are complicated and time-consuming and it is to be hoped that, in the future, some simpler method may be found yet one which preserves the right of a school to remove a pupil as a last resort and the right of a pupil to fair treatment. Of course, if a pupil commits an outrageous act — the recent rape of a girl by a boy pupil springs to mind — then there will be no need to collect evidence over a period of time. The most difficult cases are those who are constantly disruptive or defiant but not aggressive or violent.

Pastoral care and discipline 95

Use of force on pupils

Until 1987, corporal punishment was a sanction allowed in schools though it had to be administered in accordance with regulations and recorded officially. Now, as everyone knows, it has been abolished in state schools. It is still lawful in independent schools and this has been supported in a European judgement. That position may soon change and most independent schools have abandoned it anyway. The result of the publicity given to the abolition has given many teachers the impression that physical force may no longer be used in their dealings with pupils. This is not so and, indeed, in some situations if teachers did not use some reasonable physical force they might be held to be negligent.

In Chapter 2 we described an incident where two boys were fighting on a playground. A teacher separated them but did so very roughly and one boy was slightly injured. This illustrates the position over the use of physical force very well.

Physical force may not be used as a form of punishment but it may be necessary to prevent harm to the pupil or to others or to equipment or property and this is made clear in S.46 of the Education (No. 2) Act 1986. In other words, teachers may not inflict corporal punishment, though parents may still do so, but may use force in dangerous situations just as responsible parents might do.

Violence by pupils

Recently, a boy of 15 head-butted his headmistress and broke her nose. Not long before, there was an allegation of the rape of a teacher in a classroom by two pupils, and the shooting of a teacher in an independent school by a discontented pupil. Violence towards teachers has increased to such an extent that some are now carrying alarm devices.

Such attacks are criminal and any person from the age of 10 upwards may be charged with an offence, though from 10 to 14 the prosecution must show that the minor understood the nature of the crime and its wrongfulness. The illegality of a physical attack should be obvious enough.

Crimes of violence range from assault and battery to murder. An assault is action that places a person in fear of physical harm, and a battery is the unlawful physical contact that nearly always goes with it. This may then amount to actual bodily harm such as bruising or grievous bodily harm such as the breaking of bones — as in the case of the headmistress. The cutting of skin and the drawing of blood is a

96 Legal issues and the self-managing school

wounding. All these are said to be offences against the person, and possible sentences range from a conditional discharge to life imprisonment.

To maintain the confidence of staff and the good order of the school, any pupil who attacks a teacher needs to be dealt with swiftly and firmly. Immediate exclusion should normally follow and the chair of governors and police be informed. The police will take statements and pass a report to the office of the Director of Public Prosecutions where the decision whether to prosecute or not will be taken. In the event of a decision not to prosecute, the teacher concerned could bring a private prosecution, and teacher unions have been very supportive over such actions. It is to be hoped that LEAs and governors will be just as supportive.

Both governors and heads need to remember that an attack on a teacher is as serious as that on any member of the public and not a natural hazard of the job.

Summary

Each school needs a clearly defined policy over pastoral care and this needs a systematic approach in all but the smallest schools. The policy should include the definition of sanctions to be used and the formulation of school rules based on the need for good order and safety. All this should be clear and communicated to those affected by it. Legal action should be a last resort in most cases since other approaches need to be tried first. Where ill-treatment or abuse is suspected then immediate action should be taken to alert outside agencies.

11 Supervision and negligence

Schools have a legal responsibility for the supervision of pupils in their care and the basic rule is that they must act towards pupils as good reasonable parents would do. Teachers themselves are parent substitutes — that is what *in loco parentis* means — for as long as pupils remain in their charge. The concept may seem somewhat naive since parents are unlikely to have responsibility for supervising 30 or even a 1000 children and so the cases coming before the courts do take into account the professional training that teachers have received and the expertise they can be expected to show when issues of adequate supervision arise. That only adds to the concept of the responsible parent, it does not remove it. One judge put it that the test is that of the conduct of a parent who has had the benefit of a teacher's professional training.

The concept of the responsible parent is useful for teachers, however, since if something happens which such a parent could not have prevented and the teacher's expertise was not relevant then no blame can be attached.

It is not only teachers who may be *in loco parentis*. The concept applies to midday supervisors and other support staff, though the idea of professional expertise cannot be applied to them. In the most recent case on this aspect, a court decided that a caretaker who allowed older boys to practise with a shot after school was not negligent even though this was done without the school's permission.

Supervision is closely linked to the notion of *in loco parentis* and in this chapter we shall look at supervision in the classroom, around premises during breaks and on school visits, and the consequences for actions in negligence if that supervision is inadequate.

Classrooms

Here the teacher is usually in sole charge but that does not mean that the head should not give some guidance or instructions as to standards to be observed.

Incident

A class of eight-year-old pupils in a primary school is busy preparing for a parents' open evening. Some are writing, some painting and some preparing cardboard models. They are excited and interested in the work which entails the fetching and carrying of small items of equipment. The teacher is trying to co-ordinate the work and is going from child to child giving assistance. A message comes that the teacher is wanted on the telephone. Above the hubbub of activity, she tells the children to carry on with the work and behave themselves while she leaves the room for a moment. While she is out, a pupil who is making a model goes to a cupboard and takes out a pair of pointed scissors. He cuts himself.

The standard of supervision here is inadequate. A responsible parent would be unlikely to allow an eight-year-old to use or have access to scissors of this type. Because of professional training, the teacher should know that a class of young pupils should not be left unsupervised, especially when some of the activities in progress involve even a small element of risk. The scissors should not have been accessible.

Instructions from the head could include not leaving a class unsupervised except in a dire emergency, seeing that, when a number of activities are taking place these are in defined groups for ease of supervision, and insisting that potentially dangerous items are not available to pupils.

This incident took place in a primary school. Pupils in secondary schools can be expected to show a greater degree of responsibility, and understand warnings, but there are other dangers. It may not be negligent to leave pupils unsupervised in an ordinary classroom, but it could easily be so to leave them in a workshop with dangerous machines at hand.

Around premises

The head is responsible to the governors for seeing that adequate supervision is provided during breaks and lunchtimes though teachers cannot be required to supervise during the bulk of the

Supervision and negligence   99

midday break. Staff are responsible for seeing that duties allocated to them by the head during directed time are carried out and according to the head's instructions. If those instructions are inadequate then any negligence is that of the head. A failure of staff to carry out the instructions amounts to a breach of contract and could lead to disciplinary action.

During lessons, continuous supervision by the teacher is expected to be the norm though this might not apply strictly to groups of senior pupils, say, engaged in activities such as research in a school library where risks were minimal. Outside lessons and on playgrounds or around buildings, continuous supervision is not practical and the courts have recognised this. In such situations the supervision must be to quote one judge, 'reasonable and adequate in the light of the circumstances'. In practice, this means that there must be staff on patrol to spot potential hazards and be readily available to deal with any incidents that may occur. If, on a wet day, pupils were herded closely into classrooms then continuous supervision could well be expected.

The head is responsible for deciding on a list of supervision duties. This needs consultation with staff over the potential risks to be covered and then drawn up on something like the following lines:

Staff supervision duties

These duties apply to supervision before and after school sessions and during the morning breaks. The duty list for each week will be placed on the board in the staffroom on the preceding Thursday. Any member aware of non-availability to carry out a duty must inform Mr ——— before the close of school on the Friday. He will then inform substitutes personally.

These duties are all in directed time and are vital for the maintenance of good order and the safety of pupils and must be carried out as a priority over all other activities. In the event of a sudden emergency, staff may ask a colleague to deputise temporarily. Otherwise, exchange of duties is allowed but only in direct consultation with Mr ——.

Before school

Teacher 1 is on duty from 8.40 onwards, when pupils are officially allowed onto the premises, patrols outside until the bell goes and then enters school by the main entrance, encouraging latecomers to hurry up.

Teacher 2 is on duty from 8.40 onwards and patrols the inside of the school paying special attention to cloakrooms, locker areas and those rooms such as laboratories or workshops where risks are greatest. All classrooms should be locked until staff arrive.   *continued . . .*

Staff supervision duties – continued . . .

Morning break 10.30 – 10.50

Teacher 3 dismisses his/her class immediately and patrols the outside of school until relieved by teacher 5. Special attention should be given to playgrounds, areas behind the sports hall and bicycle shed, the staff car-park and the school's main exit.

Teacher 4 dismisses his/her class immediately and patrols the inside of the building until relieved by teacher 6. Special attention should be given to cloakrooms, locker areas, science laboratories, workshops and the sports hall.

At 10.40 teacher 5 relieves teacher 3 and teacher 6 relieves teacher 4. Teachers 5 and 6 continue supervision until the bell sounds at 10.50 when they encourage pupils to go to classes quickly.

Wet days

Teachers 3 and 4 together decide whether pupils should be allowed to remain inside. If so, pupils go to the main hall where they are supervised by teacher 3. Teacher 4 continues to patrol the inside of the building as before.

End of morning session 12.30 – 12.35

Teacher 1 checks that midday supervisors have reported for outside supervision duty.

Teacher 2 checks that midday supervisors have reported for inside supervision duty.

Before afternoon session 1.10 – 1.15

Teacher 3 takes over from outside midday supervisors and speeds pupils into school.

Teacher 4 takes over from inside 'midday supervisors and speeds pupils to classrooms.

After school 3.40 – 4.00

Teacher 5 patrols the outside of school ensuring that pupils on fields, playgrounds or the tennis courts have staff responsible for them and pays attention to the school's main exit.

Teacher 6 clears the inside of school making sure that pupils remaining in classrooms have staff responsible for them.

If the performance of any of these duties highlights particular problems, they should be reported to Mr ——.

This model has virtues which need to be applied to all such lists though it may be overcomplicated for smaller schools.

- It emphasises that these are important compulsory contractual duties in directed time.

Supervision and negligence 101

- The entire day is covered from the moment that pupils have a right to be on the premises until they should have left. Duties for midday supervisors would have to be issued to fit in.
- Although there is some flexibility here, and there is an allowance for staff breaks, a casual approach to duties is not allowed and plenty of warning is given.
- Attention is paid to the end of sessions — often ignored by some schools.
- There is provision for wet days.
- Emphasis is placed on dangerous areas.
- Staff are encouraged to spot problems and report them.

It needs to be added that the performance of these duties should be monitored closely by senior staff or by the head and kept under constant review in the light of changing circumstances. The head should see that the governors are aware of the staff supervision duties that are in force.

Off the premises

Parents have a right to expect that pupils will be on the premises and supervised during school sessions. If pupils remain for school lunch then they have a right to expect supervision. If, in either of these circumstances, pupils are to be off the school premises then the consent of parents should be obtained. The exception to this is if pupils are taken, say, to a swimming bath under direct supervision or are escorted to a nearby sports field for games lessons.

What if pupils are to be off the premises on a number of occasions when continuous direct supervision is not possible, say for research purposes as part of an examination project? It would be unreasonable for parental consent to be obtained for each occasion so the position should be explained, details given, the nature of the supervision described, and consent obtained for a sequence of visits. If the parents refuse then the pupil should not be allowed off the premises.

The greatest risks will be presented by school visits. When things go wrong the attention of the media and the public outcry can be very damaging to the school concerned let alone the traumatic effect on pupils, parents and staff. It has to be said that, when major accidents do occur — as in the Cairngorms, in Austria, at Land's End and most recently at Lyme Regis — there is almost always evidence of lack of planning for emergencies, lack of monitoring or inadequate supervision. Complacency is usually at the root of the problem — things have always gone smoothly before.

102 Legal issues and the self-managing school

Each visit needs to be looked at afresh, no matter how many times similar ones have taken place previously. If we examine one situation, we can bring out important aspects and action that needs to be taken.

Llangollen and back

A member of the staff of the Waterway School is a fanatic over boat-building and canal cruising. Under his guidance the school has built two canal cruisers and he has taken pupils on several camping trips using the boats as transport. Now he proposes during a holiday period to take a mixed party of 15 pupils, aged from 14 to 17, on a week's trip to Llangollen and back. This route has not been covered before.

Sleeping on the boats for such a party is not possible and the idea is to carry camping equipment aboard which will be used for each overnight stop. Two canoes will also be carried. The activities planned will include bird-watching and recording, sketching, mapping, canoeing and visiting places of interest en route. Only pupils who can swim will be taken.

---

1. *Approval needs to be obtained from the head and governors and arrangements need to be in line with the school's stated policies over visits including the provision of insurance.*

2. *The leader needs to be aware of what has to be negotiated.* The route may be obvious from a map but the conditions on the ground need checking. If this is not possible by boat then two or three towpath walks could probably cover the distance.

3. *The leader needs to decide on the activities to be included and the potential risks involved.* Most here seem reasonably safe except for the canoeing. Canals may be mostly shallow but there are deep sections. Only pupils who are competent swimmers should be allowed to use the canoes even though canal water can hardly be said to be rough. The canoes should not be used at all unless one of the accompanying staff is a qualified canoeing instructor. The canoeists should wear life-jackets and so should other pupils when travelling on the boats.

   What other risks might there be? It seems unlikely that all 15 pupils and staff can travel during the day on two boats laden with camping equipment. What about the supervision of those on towpaths or elsewhere? Other hazards might include the use of cooking stoves in or near tents, the handling of engines and fuel or the working of the locks.

4. *The level of staffing needs to be decided upon.* If things go really wrong, the group could be at some distance from even a village. They will be engaged in different activities, possibly meeting at the next overnight stop. Although there are only 15 older pupils involved, at least three staff would seem neces-

Supervision and negligence

sary, though two staff accompanied by several responsible parents might suffice. The party is a mixed one so an adult female must be included.

5. *Equipment needs to be asssessed and checked.* This would include canoes, boats, life-jackets, camping equipment, fire appliances and first-aid equipment.

6. *Information for parents would need to be given well beforehand and their written consent obtained.* The information should include dates and times, a map of the route including overnight stops, the activities to be undertaken, the extent of supervision to be provided, and the name and number of the co-ordinator back at home.

7. *Information from parents would be required.* This should include details of any known medical condition that may be relevant and the telephone number of a relative or friend to be contacted if parents should be out or away. Parents should be asked to certify the pupil's competence at swimming.

8. *Contacts with a co-ordinator at home need to be available.* This needs to be a responsible person who has all details of the trip with a list of pupils and adults involved and their home addresses and telephone numbers.

The preparation for this trip would involve a deal of work and would be time-consuming but that is necessary in the interests of safety and the peace of mind of parents and staff. Accidents can happen, of course, but careful planning and forethought should make them very rare indeed and if they could not have been avoided then there is no negligence.

Negligence

It is when an accident could have been avoided that actions in negligence are likely to be brought. However, the chance of success in such actions under English law is limited and there is at present no legal aid available in such cases. If the negligence is obvious then usually the defendant will be only too willing to settle out of court in order to minimise legal costs. If the offer of compensation is not considered good enough then the plaintiff may decide to go to court.

Most actions in negligence reach court because the defendant believes the plaintiff cannot prove the necessary elements of negligence and thus hopes to avoid any liability.

Negligence is a tort — a civil wrong. It occurs when harm is caused to others by careless action or careless inaction. In all but obvious

104 Legal issues and the self-managing school

cases the plaintiff must prove four things: that a duty of care existed towards him or her; that the duty of care was broken; that damage occurred; and that the damage was reasonably foreseeable, i.e. that the defendant knew, or ought reasonably to have known, that such harm could occur.

There are defences to a negligence action such as that the accident was inevitable, no reasonable care could have prevented it. Another, applicable to school situations, is that of consent. A person who freely consents to run a risk of harm cannot succeed in an action if the damage is clearly a result of running that risk — injuries on sports fields for instance. This can raise interesting cases. In one, a pupil was injured when tackled by a teacher during a game of rugby and was awarded damages because there was no consent to the risk of being tackled by a hefty male teacher. The same injury inflicted by a fellow pupil would have led to a different result and, indeed, did so in a separate case where no compensation was awarded. There was consent to the possible injury by another pupil.

We now turn to the Llangollen trip again and discover that, in spite of all the thought and preparation, two accidents did happen. In the light of what has just been said regarding negligence, what might be the result?

Jake

The Llangollen canal is very shallow in most parts. One of the boats became stuck so Jake volunteered to jump onto the towpath and push the boat off. This he did but the boat came away quicker than he anticipated and he slid into the water, cutting his leg rather badly on a piece of scrap iron under the surface. He was sent to hospital by ambulance and received a number of stitches.

Jessica

At one of the overnight stops Jessica was cooking for herself and two friends. It was windy and so she took her stove into her tent though, at the start of the trip, all the pupils had been told not do this. The tent caught fire and Jessica received severe burns. Luckily, a farm was near the site and an ambulance arrived quickly.

If we apply the tests for negligence to Jake's case we find that, of course, his supervisors owed him a duty of care — they had to be concerned for his welfare. For teachers, breach of that duty of care means not acting as a responsible parent or behaving unprofessionally. Would a parent allow his son of 14 or so to push a boat off the bank of a shallow canal? Probably yes. There is physical damage here. Could the accident have been foreseen? It seems very doubtful. There

Supervision and negligence

is no strong case for an action in negligence since two of the tests do not seem to have been satisfied.

If we apply the tests to Jessica, we have to say that there may well be breach of the duty of care. No responsible parent or teacher in charge of an expedition would allow the use of a stove inside a tent. On the other hand, Jessica has been warned and is old enough to understand what the danger is. Probably an adult should have supervised the cooking more carefully. Certainly, there is damage here and that damage is foreseeable if stoves are used inside a tent. There may be grounds for an action here but, even if successful, the amount of damages would be likely to be reduced because of Jessica's contributory negligence. She ought to have known the risk she was taking and she disobeyed instructions.

Probably there were no further trips to Llangollen.

Summary

Schools have a legal obligation to provide adequate supervision of pupils according to the particular circumstances in question. The basic position is that teachers must act as responsible parents would do but also bearing in mind the higher standard they should observe because of their professional training. That standard may vary according to factors such as the age of pupils, their capacity to understand, the numbers involved, the nature of the activity, the risks involved, the inherent dangers of the equipment, the physical surroundings, the weather conditions even. Each instance requires separate consideration.

When supervision has to be provided over a long period, it needs monitoring and regular review. Duties in such situations need to be clearly defined. Special attention needs to be given to activities off the school site.

If due care is taken then liability for negligence is unlikely and negligence is hard to prove. Accidents do happen, they don't necessarily lead to legal action and compensation.

As we saw in an earlier chapter, employers are vicariously liable for the negligence of their employees while acting within their scope of employment. The governors of Waterway school approved the Llangollen trip so, even though it took place during the holidays, the staff were acting as employees.

12 Premises and health and safety

Although they receive finance from an LEA, aided and special agreement schools have always been responsible for the management and control of their premises since their governors were the employers and they, or the trustees, owned the school and its grounds. Controlled schools had limited powers over their premises, although they were not the employers of staff. Other schools were largely controlled by the LEA, which could dictate over the use of school premises. One of the results of grant-maintained status is that the governors obtain full control of the use of premises and are, in effect, the owners. The consequence of giving delegated powers to the governors of other schools has been to place them in a similar position, though there are still some grey areas. We now therefore have the situation where governors of all schools control the use of their premises — which includes grounds as well as buildings.

No longer will LEA regulations over the use and control of schools apply generally. The freedom thus given to schools to decide on minor building works (major ones are not included for controlled and county schools), to decide on maintenance and cleaning, and on the use of schools by outsiders sounds interesting but it entails a great deal of planning and thought by governing bodies and it raises a number of legal issues. The consequences of breaches of the law are now most likely to fall on governing bodies rather than on the LEA.

We can best examine problems and issues that may arise by looking at a week in a busy school — the Everyman School — which encourages the involvement of parents, and fosters links with the surrounding community. Like most schools of its type, at the end of each week it issues a bulleting to all staff and pupils giving details of events for the next week and any other notices of importance.

Premises and health and safety

Everyman School bulletin
Week commencing Monday December 10th

Important
During this week contractors will be resurfacing the tennis courts. This area is out of bounds to all pupils until further notice. Please keep away from this area and from all equipment used by the contractors.

Monday
The school basketball team will be playing in the area final against the Allsuch School in the sports hall at 7 pm. Spectators welcome.

Tuesday and Wednesday
The local dramatic society, the Byway Players, will be presenting 'A Christmas Carol' in the main hall at 7.30 pm. Tickets half-price (50p) for pupils, obtainable at the school office, or at the door on the night.

Thursday
A fire drill will be held at some time during the school day. Follow carefully the instructions given to you and leave the building as quickly as possible.

An exhibition of work by pupils will be held in the Art department from 7 – 9 pm. All welcome. No entry fee.

Saturday
The PTA Christmas Fair will be held in the main hall and nearby classrooms. Doors open at 2 pm. Entry for children under 16 and OAPs 20p. Others 50p. All proceeds towards the replacement of the minibus. Persuade the whole family to come.

Ice and snow
The cold weather is now upon us. In early mornings there could well be icy patches on school paths or playgrounds. The caretaker will salt these wherever possible but pupils must take care and sliding on paths is not allowed. Should there be snow then any snowballing must only take place on the school field, not on playgrounds or near school buildings.

First aid
There have been several instances recently of pupils hurting themselves in break-times and not reporting injuries to staff. Even if the cut or bruise seems to be just a minor one, you must report it and get first-aid treatment.

Trespassing
Pupils are asked to see that relatives or friends who are not members of the school do not come onto the premises without obtaining permission from the school office first. If they fail to do this then they are trespassing. *continued . . .*

108 Legal issues and the self-managing school

Everyman School bulletin – continued . . .
Evening classes
Pupils in Years 11, 12 and 13 are eligible to join classes commencing in
January and these are free to those pupils. Prospectuses available from
the school office.

Occupier's liability

Legal responsibility for those who come onto school premises may be
civil or criminal. The civil responsibility is to be found in the law
relating to negligence and in two Acts: the Occupier's Liability Act
1957 and the Occupier's Liability Act 1984. The first lays down a
common duty of care towards all those who have direct or implied
permission to be on premises, and the second extends this duty
including a duty to show concern for known trespassers or where
trespassing is likely to occur, especially where young children are
concerned. This does not mean that an occupier is always liable for
injuries caused to trespassers but that reasonable steps must be taken
to prevent the trespassing and that hazards must not be created for the
specific purpose of harming those who trespass.

In the last chapter we explained negligence as a tort, a civil wrong,
and, in effect, the two Acts mentioned here place negligence towards
those on premises on a statutory basis.

The occupier of premises is usually the owner and this is the
position with aided, special agreement and grant-maintained schools.
It may be so in the case of controlled schools but, for other schools, the
owner is the LEA. That seems to make the LEA the occupier but, in
the light of controls and powers given to governing bodies where
LEAs have ceased to be able to dictate over the management of
internal affairs, that seems to be unrealistic. This is a legal problem yet
to be solved. In any case, LEAs and governors, either singly or jointly,
must see that proper insurance cover is provided for claims over
negligence with regard to the use of premises.

If we turn to the weekly bulletin for the Everyman School we can
identify a number of situations where the school may have responsibilities or difficulties with regard to occupier's liability:

- It has to face all the hazards of the normal school day since all
  pupils, staff and legitimate outsiders are covered by the two
  Acts. There could be hazards over slippery conditions and the
  school must take reasonable steps to guard against these.
  Snowballing can be dangerous but to ban it altogether seems
  unreasonable and probably unenforceable anyway but there

Premises and health and safety 109

are steps here to limit the risks. The fire drill will have to be properly planned, carried out and assessed (this will be discussed again later) and there may be problems created by the outside contractors.

- The position over outside firms coming onto school premises to carry out work is that the school owes them a duty of care in one sense. The school could be liable if workmen are injured by some defect or hazard that had been created for them or had not been pointed out. On the other hand, specialists are expected to be aware of risks normally associated with their particular line of work and guard against them. If a teacher driving the school minibus backs into a workman and injures him then the school will be liable: if the workman is injured by hot tar escaping during the resurfacing then any negligence is that of his employer who must carry insurance for such events. The contractor might also be liable for injuries to pupils caused by misuse of equipment or failure to take reasonable care.

- Outside normal hours, this school has allowed a large number of people to come onto its premises as legitimate visitors. They include spectators at the basketball match, the audience at the play, visitors to the art exhibition and those coming to the Christmas Fair. There is an inference also that evening classes may also be in progress. A duty of care is owed to all of them. Defective equipment in the sports hall, inadequate fire arrangements or unsafe seating at the play, a slippery floor in an Art room, some accident at the Christmas Fair or in a room where an evening class is in progress could all lead to accusations of negligence though readers will remember the difficulty of proof in negligence actions.

- Of course, all those at the school, either during the day or after school hours, have consented to run some risks and cannot succeed in negligence if what happens is a possible result of running that risk. All pupils run the risks inherent in school lessons and activities — accidents on the sports fields or playgrounds, injuries from misuse of safe equipment, a fall that no one could have prevented. A spectator runs some risk in watching the basketball match — if a ball strikes him in the eye and causes damage then he has no claim.

- A person has no cause for action if he or she exceeds the purpose for which entry was authorised. A visitor to the art exhibition who then wandered off into another area of the school and was injured in some way would have no case.

110 Legal issues and the self-managing school

Health and safety

The Health and Safety at Work Act 1974, as amended and developed by succeeding legislation, is a part of the criminal law. It applies to all places where work is carried on and therefore to schools. It does not just apply to staff who work in them. It also applies to all who are on the premises with direct or implied permission for legitimate purposes. Therefore at the Everyman it covers pupils, teaching and support staff, spectators at the basketball match, playgoers, visitors to the art exhibition and the Christmas Fair and those attending evening classes, as well as any casual visitors during the school day.

The legislation, though criminal, is not intended as a means of bringing numerous prosecutions, and it is not meant to expect perfect compliance with all details. It is intended to make employers aware of their obligations and to do whatever is reasonable for the safety of those at places of work:

> ' . . . the duty of every employer to ensure, as far as is reasonably practicable, the health, safety and welfare at work of all his employees.'

Employees have responsibilities under the legislation too — they must take care in their work and obey the reasonable instructions of employers with regard to health and safety matters. An employee can be prosecuted — though, to the best of the writer's knowledge, there has only ever been one prosecution of a teacher and none of a governing body. There have been a number of prosecutions of chief education officers. However, prosecution of the employer may well raise problems in the future. In aided and grant-maintained schools the position is clear enough — the governors are the employer and may be prosecuted. In other schools the LEA is still technically the employer and so may be prosecuted but, since their governors have been given wide powers over the control of premises, it is becoming unreasonable for the LEA to know what is happening, impose decisions and take action. A likely outcome in the future is for each governing body to become liable for health and safety provision in its school.

The legal requirements are to be found in the 1974 Act and Regulations which follow. A Regulation is in the form of a statutory instrument and so it is legally binding. Recent directives from the EC have added further weight to the already complex law on the subject. The primary legislation is followed by numerous Codes of Practice.

Premises and health and safety 111

Most of these are not legally binding but failure to follow their guidance as far as possible could be construed as acting unreasonably.

Responsibility for health and safety matters lies with the Health and Safety Commission which operates through the Health and Safety Executive and its inspectors. They have extensive powers. They may issue orders prohibiting certain procedures or the use of certain equipment. They may issue improvement notices whereby an employer is given a certain time in which to put matters right. They are entitled to receive reports of accidents or 'dangerous occurrences' in places of work and may decide to investigate such reports.

In case all this suggests a 'big brother' approach and a rigid bureaucracy, it has to be said that the approach of the inspectors is usually helpful, the purpose being to encourage employers to be more aware of dangers and to provide better conditions by following advice.

Health and Safety is now such a complex area of the law that it merits a book to itself and it is not possible to deal with it here in detail. The most important approaches to it for schools may be summarised thus:

The governing body

The governors must formulate and keep under review a policy regarding the school's approach to health and safety matters.

Health and safety committee

Each school needs to establish such a committee to deal with health and safety matters. The head should always be a member. Governors also need to be represented on it because of the responsibilities laid upon them. The remaining membership should be wide. Teaching staff need to be included because of their knowledge of the building and of the possible behaviour, or misbehaviour, of pupils. The caretaker and a midday supervisor could also be very helpful, as could a parent with some specialist knowledge of this aspect of employment. It might be useful to include a senior pupil.

The functions of the committee would need to be defined but they should certainly include the assessment of risks, the monitoring of health and safety provision, and the making of recommendations to the head and governing body. The formation of such a committee is not yet a legal requirement but it is highly desirable. The committee has no legal liability.

Safety representative

The appointment of safety representatives at the request of recognised

112 Legal issues and the self-managing school

unions is a legal requirement. As each union in a school is entitled to a representative, there could be enough of them to form the committee mentioned above. In practice, unions usually agree to nominate one person to represent all of them. The safety representative should be a valuable member of the committee on safety. He/she is expected to be aware of the requirements of the legislation, undertake training (reasonable time off work must be given for this), monitor risks and keep the head and committee informed. The safety representative has no more legal responsibility than any other member of staff.

Assessment of risks

A fundamental aspect of the school's policy should be to assess the risks that are present, both in routine matters and occasional activities such as school visits, and this seems a useful initial task for the committee. It could start by listing actions already taken to provide safety — staff supervision duties and fire drills would be examples. It could then identify serious risks not catered for and make suggestions, following this by an assessment of lesser risks. The bulletin here reveals risks over icy paths and snowballing and these could be addressed. All this would be a time-consuming process but the work could be shared by a number of individuals with the results being drawn up into a comprehensive statement, subject to periodic review and forming part of the school's general policy.

Particular risks

While most of the risks for pupils and staff may seem obvious enough, since they have existed for many years, there are some which need particular attention because they are relatively new. For example, most schools were built before the need for extensive car-parking or the use of school minibuses. Computers, televisions, videos and other items of electrical equipment now proliferate. Machinery in workshops, apparatus in laboratories and in gymnasia are all more complex and perhaps dangerous than in the past. The risks presented must be considered.

Environmental factors

Ventilation, light and circulation are all health and safety matters. So is workspace and here the Education (School Premises) Regulations 1981 come into consideration over teaching spaces. There are new

Premises and health and safety 113

regulations regarding visual display units which are likely to affect office staff, though probably not pupils. Employers must pay for eye tests in these circumstances and supply corrective spectacles if necessary.

Training

While training for safety representatives must be allowed, there is no such provision for other staff. Since teachers and support staff, particularly midday supervisors, are in such responsible positions, it does seem advisable for them to have some training and this could easily form the programme of a training day in directed time.

Reports

For its own sake, a school needs to keep a log of accidents or injuries that occur, first-aid or hospital treatment given and action taken to prevent a repetition where that was possible. There is also a legal requirement under the Reporting of Injuries, Diseases and Dangerous Occurrences Regulations 1985 on employers to submit reports on a prescribed form of serious items to the Health and Safety Executive. The head is responsible for seeing that this is done. In aided and grant-maintained schools the report should be sent direct. In voluntary and county schools there may well still exist a system whereby the reports are sent to the LEA, which will have an officer responsible for health and safety matters and who will decide whether the reports should be passed on to the HSE.

Guidance is given under the regulations as to the kind of injuries, diseases and dangerous occurrences that should be reported. Those leading to the death within a year of an employee, pupil or visitor form one category. Another is a major injury such as a serious fracture, loss of sight of an eye or one that causes the injured person to be kept in hospital for more than 24 hours. A third is an incident which causes an employee to be off work immediately for three days or more.

The diseases listed are largely concerned with industry and not applicable to schools — those relevant to staff and pupils, such as meningitis or tuberculosis, are the concern of the local Medical Officer of Health.

Dangerous occurrences are those such as fire, explosion, collapse of part of the building or escape of a dangerous substance. Any of these should be reported even if no one suffers harm.

The head may have some difficulty in deciding what to report. The best advice is to be on the safe side and to submit a report when

114 Legal issues and the self-managing school

any incident seems relatively serious and especially when it is caused by faulty equipment, some building defect or a lack of proper supervision. Accidents that occur on school visits should not be forgotten.

Everyman again

If that school had a safety committee which had made an assessment of risks then those of the week we examined might run as follows:

- Equipment in the sports hall. Is this in safe condition and has it received its annual safety check?
- Arrangements in the main hall for drama productions. Is the stage lighting in good order and has it been subjected to regular checks? Is the fire-fighting equipment in good order? Is the nearest alarm working? Is there proper provision for emergency lighting, safe seating, exit signs and clear escape routes in case of fire? Have fire officers inspected and made any suggestions? Have the requirements of a public entertainment licence been met?
- Arrangements for dealing with emergencies when the school is in use outside normal school hours. Are clear escape routes and fire-fighting equipment available for an event such as the Christmas Fair? Is the alarm working? It is Saturday remember. Are students at evening classes aware of the action to be taken in case of fire? What are the arrangements for the provision of first-aid in such circumstances?
- Fire drill. See below.

Fire drill

Although arson committed while schools are empty has been on the increase for a number of years, the incidence of fire while a school is in session is still a rare event. This, in itself, is dangerous because of the risk of complacency. Of all risks in a large building full of busy people, and young people at that, fire is the most serious. Yet, to date, schools are not even required to have a fire certificate unless the premises are used under a public entertainment licence.

Each school needs to have clear arrangements to deal with outbreaks of fire. These need to be drawn up carefully — another useful task for the safety committee — and not by the head alone. The governors need to approve the arrangements which should be reviewed at least annually — more often if problems arise. Those

Premises and health and safety

arrangements should include the positioning and regular inspection of fire-fighting equipment, the siting and regular testing of alarms, action by those discovering a fire, responsibility for calling the fire service and procedures for speedy evacuation — the fire drill.

The drill at Everyman is to be held with warning given, although the time is not stated. Drills should also be held without warning and should, at times, include a test of coping with an unexpected hazard — say the blocking of one exit. Perhaps this is the third drill held at Everyman during the first term of the academic year. The first would have been in September, with warning, to test the routine; the second in October, without warning, to test immediate reactions; and the third in December with additional hazard added. Perhaps, after that, two drills a term would suffice.

While immediate attempts to put out a fire seem reasonable enough, the approach should always be to clear the building as quickly as possible and remove everyone from danger even if that means the building is destroyed. Buildings can be replaced.

Here is a basic checklist that the Everyman committee might use in planning its fire drill:

- Appropriate siting of equipment and alarms. All working.
- Action defined for all to take, including responsibility for making the 999 call.
- Identifying the main escape exits. Escape routes for each area defined and based on a close study of the geography of the school and patterns of movement. Alternative routes provided for each area.
- Instructions for each area posted prominently in that area and explained to pupils by staff.
- Assembly points identified with arrangements for the provision of registers and carrying out checks.
- Arrangements for staff in non-teaching areas such as kitchens or offices.
- Attendance of fire officer, if possible, to comment and advise.
- Record of time taken and difficulties that occurred.
- Review of drill and changes made as necessary.

First-aid

If fire is a rare occurrence then giving first-aid or other medical attention in a school is not. The basic position of teachers in such matters is that they must again act towards pupils as responsible parents would do. That is really a matter of common-sense, not of medical expertise or knowledge. A good parent would give treatment

116   Legal issues and the self-managing school

over minor cuts or bruises but would seek expert medical attention if
there was a suspicion of a need for stitching or X-ray. Schools and
teachers must do the same.

Strictly speaking, the legislation under health and safety regarding
first-aid does not apply to pupils but it does to employees so schools
must have first-aid provision and naturally this is extended to pupils.
Where there are 50 or more employees at a school, there must be a
trained first aider and for those with fewer employees there must be an
'appointed person'. That person need not have training in first-aid,
though that would be helpful, but is responsible for taking charge
when an accident occurs and calling swiftly for specialist help. The
regulations also deal with the availability and contents of first-aid
boxes.

Teachers are often very concerned over their position with regard
to first-aid and the provision of drugs. Here are answers to the most
common queries:

1. If I give first-aid and this turns out to be wrong, am I in
    trouble?

    You are required to act as a good parent and parents can be
    wrong. If your treatment seems sound on grounds of
    common-sense, you have little to fear provided that, if there is
    any doubt, you have obtained expert help as soon as possible.
    Even if negligence was to be proved, your employer is
    vicariously liable for your actions.

2. If pupils seem to have had a bad fall on the playground or
    field, should I bring them inside?

    No. Be reluctant even to touch them. Cover them with
    something warm until expert help arrives.

3. I know that parents should be informed as soon as possible in
    a case that may be serious. What if they cannot be contacted
    or if they are late in coming?

    Call an ambulance first and then contact the parents, they can
    always follow later. Swift treatment is the paramount con-
    sideration.

4. If a pupil is taken away by ambulance, should a teacher go as
    well?

    If there is a responsible adult available to accompany the
    pupil, not necessarily a teacher, then that is ideal but it must
    not be at the expense of proper supervision of other pupils.

5. Can I be required to take custody of drugs and give them to
    pupils during the school day?

Premises and health and safety

117

No. You can refuse. If you do consent then make sure that they are kept under lock and key and not overnight. Remember that, if you assume responsibility for them, and by your carelessness they fall into the wrong hands, you could be accused of negligence.

Everyman further

If we look once again at the week's bulletin for the school, we can find further examples of where legal issues may arise over the use of the school's premises. These include licensing for dramatic performances and the consumption of alcohol; raffles and the serving of refreshments at the Christmas Fair; and the general problem of trespassing that seems to exist.

'The Christmas Carol'

This is put on by a local drama group so they are responsible for permission from the agents to perform. If they wish to have a bar serving alcohol during the interval then they may obtain a licence from the local magistrates' court. Groups such as dramatic societies or PTAs may obtain three such occasional licences during any one year and they are responsible for proper conduct of the bar, which is open to police inspection.

The school also has responsibilities. The governors have the power to decide on the use of premises by outside groups and the charges payable. This creates something akin to a contractual situation — the school providing reasonable facilities in return for payment. The governors could lay down any conditions they wished. In any case, charge or not, the school would have to note the following:

- A licence for the performance of plays would have to be obtained and the school would be responsible for this. It applies whenever the general public are admitted, whether payment is required or not. It does not apply to school plays where entry is restricted to pupils and to close relatives.
- The licence is obtainable from the local council office and will contain conditions relating to audience numbers, seating and fire precautions. A fire certificate must be granted. The school, not the drama group, must see that the conditions are met.
- Although the conduct of the bar is in the hands of the society, if the school knowingly allows the terms of the licence to be

118   Legal issues and the self-managing school

broken — the caretaker permitting after-hours drinking, for
example — then it could also be liable. The head would need
to check arrangements with the society.

The law is similar over the licensing of schools for music and
dancing.

The Christmas Fair

No licence is required for this. The conditions over occupier's liability
and health and safety, already discussed, will apply but there will also
be the question of lotteries.

Lotteries held during the event in the form of raffles require no
permission though there must be no money prizes, the draw must be
held at the time, and all proceeds must go to the organisation and not
to individuals.

It is likely that the PTA will have organised a Christmas draw on a
much wider basis with the tickets sold outside school to the general
public and the prizes to be drawn at the Fair. If that is so then
registration with the local authority is necessary, and compliance with
the conditions laid down. Cash prizes are then permitted.

Trespass

A trespasser is a person who has no direct or implied right to be on
property or one who has a right of entry but who behaves in such a way
as to abuse that right — a member of the audience at the play who
drinks deeply during the interval and then climbs onto the stage
during the second half of the performance, disrupting the actors. He
had a right of entry by buying his ticket but then abused that right by
his behaviour.

Trespassers are usually very difficult to deal with since normally
trespass is a civil matter and the police have no powers unless some
other conduct takes place such as criminal damage or assault. The
civil remedies for trespass are a court injunction forbidding future
entry or ejection by the use of reasonable force — neither very
satisfactory. Therefore a notice saying, 'Trespassers will be prosecuted' has very little significance.

Fortunately, this is no longer true for schools. S.40 of the Local
Government (Miscellaneous Provisions) Act 1982 reads:

> Any person who without lawful authority is present on premises to
> which this section applies and causes or permits nuisance or
> disturbance to the annoyance of persons who lawfully use those
> premises (whether or not such persons are present at the time)

Premises and health and safety 119

shall be guilty of an offence and shall be liable on summary conviction to a fine not exceeding £50.

So there is now a criminal offence of trespass on educational premises. The police have power to act though the offence is not an arrestable one.

The offender needs to be told by an authorised person that he or she is a trespasser and must leave. Governors may designate authorised persons and the head is an obvious one. It is useful to name the caretaker and, at the Everyman School for example, someone in charge of premises during the evening. A rowdy spectator at the basketball match, or a difficult parent, could be dealt with by this law.

The prosecution may be brought by the governors of aided or grant-maintained schools or the LEA in the case of other schools. The police may also initiate a prosecution.

Incident

An ex-pupil had a girl-friend in Year 11 of a secondary school. He was unemployed and had taken to coming on school premises during breaks and lunchtimes to talk to her. The head had told him twice that he was trespassing and he had left without any trouble. One lunchtime he came onto the playground again and when told to leave by a midday supervisor he swore at her. By the time the head arrived he had vanished again.

The police were informed and the youth was prosecuted and fined £35 with costs. As he was 17, the details and his name and address were printed in the local paper.

Summary

Governors are responsible for the control and use of their school's premises, and must have a policy for the health and safety of those who lawfully use them. Under the civil law of occupier's liability, they owe those users a common duty of care. The school needs to keep under review all aspects of safety, and to pay particular attention to fire hazards and high risk areas. Standards of perfection are not expected but the school needs to be able to show that all reasonable precautions and actions have been taken.

13 Financial matters

It is assumed to be a great advantage under the new legislation for schools to be able to manage their own finances and, indeed, for many schools this will be the case. Both grant-maintained and other schools have a right to receive certain finance from the LEA which must, to a large degree, be related to the number of pupils on roll. Control of finance means that each school may decide on its own priorities though, for small schools, there is little room for manoeuvre once staffing costs have been met. The responsibility, and extra work, placed on heads and governing bodies is great and especially worrying as most are inexperienced and untrained over budgeting and accounting. Some politicians seem to assume naively that it is a matter of simple housekeeping.

Grant-maintained schools have the wider powers and, already, there have been instances of such schools running into serious financial difficulties over their failure to cope. In one instance this led to a large deficit, the dismissal of a number of teachers and the resignation of the head. Other schools must comply with the provisions for budgeting, accounting and auditing set out in the local LMS scheme produced by the LEA and this does ensure guidelines for the actual handling of finance. If that handling breaks down then the LEA may take over. If it breaks down in grant-maintained schools then the more remote DFE must intervene.

Apart from the need to handle finances in an efficient and open manner, which may avoid any suggestion of malpractice or incompetence, there are legal issues that may arise. If we examine the discussions of one group of governors, we can identify some of them.

The governors (County School)

Several of the governors are hard-headed businessmen who are used to handling financial problems in their working lives. They are members of the school's finance committee and, before the next

Financial matters   121

meeting, they get together to gather ideas as to ways of saving money or raising extra finance since the school is finding it almost impossible to balance its budget. They come to the meeting with suggestions to be discussed with the head.

They believe that the school is overstaffed and, since salaries form the greatest expenditure, they propose that two teachers should be made redundant. They believe that they have discovered a firm of industrial cleaners who would carry out the regular cleaning of the premises at a much cheaper rate than the present firm. Perhaps higher charges could be made for school visits. The school operates a minibus for which no charge is made to pupils — modest charges could bring in a substantial amount over an academic year. Perhaps charges could be made for pupils taking examinations in more than a stated number of subjects. Outside bodies use the school for a very small fee. Such use could be charged at a more realistic rate.

At the meeting, they put these suggestions to the head who then has to explain the position with regard to each one.

Staff dismissal

The governors have the right to appoint, discipline and dismiss staff. If the governors of grant-maintained or aided schools decide to make staff redundant then, if those staff are awarded compensation for unfair dismissal by an industrial tribunal, the governors must pay. For other schools, the LEA must pay unless it can show that the governors have acted unreasonably or unfairly, in which case the amount of the compensation can be deducted from the school's budget. Here, if the governors do finally decide to make two staff redundant, they must consult the LEA and go through the agreed procedures. The head needs to explain this.

Contracts for services

Governors can make contracts for services but they cannot change the contracts in such a simple fashion. Under the Local Government Act 1988 services for catering, cleaning and general maintenance must be put out to competitive tender. The governors are free to make contracts for other matters and may well save money in a number of directions. Of course, the general rules of contract will always apply.

Charging

The governors are required to have a charging and remissions policy which states when charges are to be made and where remissions are allowed, for example, where the parents are in receipt of income support or family credit benefit. Charges may not be made for education nor for books or equipment. Charges may be made for individual music tuition. Charges may not be made for visits in connection with public examinations or where the greater proportion of the visit is in normal schooltime though parents may make voluntary contributions. Reasonable charges may be made when the visit takes place largely out of school time so a theatre visit where the party left half an hour before school ended would qualify. The governors cannot raise finance here.

Minibus

If it is proposed to make charges for travel in the minibus then the vehicle must be registered under the Transport Act 1985 and a permit obtained, either through the LEA or direct from the Traffic Commissioners. The vehicle must comply with strict requirements laid down by the legislation. The charges made must be on a non-profit making basis where the payments reflect a reasonable charge to cover running costs and depreciation. The charges here could certainly help to cover costs relating to the minibus.

Examination entries

While it may be possible to restrict the number of examinations taken by pupils for educational reasons, normally no charges may be made for what are known as prescribed subjects as stated under the Education Reform Act 1988. These include all subjects at A-Level and at GCSE. The governors can charge for examinations and for subjects outside this list, and where pupils are entered for a second examination in the same subject. They may also charge the fees for examinations where pupils fail to arrive for an examination without a reasonable excuse, so governors may be able to raise a little extra finance in this way.

Use by outside bodies

Here the governors are in a stronger position. They have the right to control the use of premises outside normal school sessions and meal-breaks and so may decide who should use the school facilities and what charges should be made. It is perfectly reasonable for these to be realistic and to bring in some income to assist with expenses over heating, lighting and cleaning.

Financial matters 123

Unofficial funds

All schools have to deal with money that does not come from official sources and yet the head is responsible to the governing body, and it to parents, for seeing that such finance is handled with efficiency and with scrupulous honesty.

There may be a scheme whereby the parents of each pupil make a voluntary contribution each term to a general school fund. This should be accounted for separately and carefully, and a balance sheet produced for the governing body, staff and any parents wishing to inspect it. It is likely that this will be a general welfare fund which gives assistance to pupils from deprived backgrounds so names should rarely be recorded in the open statements. It would be advisable to state clearly the general purposes of such a fund. It should be set up in a proper manner with a bank account and normal completion of cheques, with at least two signatures from three nominations.

Where money is collected for other purposes, such as for school visits, separate accounts need to be kept and schools are often careless over this. The following guidelines could serve for any such visit and put the head and governors in a position to answer any criticism from parents:

- Cost clearly stated in the general details given to parents and itemised if necessary.
- Costs always slightly overestimated. Refunds are always accepted with pleasure, not so demands for further payment.
- A receipt given to pupils or parents whenever money is paid.
- Money paid through one main school fund and staff given a receipt for their payments. No separate accounts in the names of individual members of staff.
- After the visit, a balance sheet presented to the head by the staff responsible for the visit and then placed on file for any inspection by parents or governors on request.
- An indication that any surplus will result in a refund unless the amount left is too small to be divided. It would then be transferred to the general welfare fund.

Unofficial funds should be properly audited by independent outsiders and not by members of staff or the governing body.

Most parents trust teachers, and most teachers are honest and trustworthy, but there needs to be evidence of that honesty and the impression of care and efficiency over the handling of other people's money. When theft or fraud is suspected, it can do great harm to the confidence of parents and to the local image of the school.

124 Legal issues and the self-managing school

Finally, it must be said that the person in the best position to mishandle money and remain undiscovered until a major crisis occurs is the head. The head should never be involved personally in the collection or handling of money. He or she should be always in a position to check the handling of it by others if that should prove necessary.

Other sources

There are at least two other ways in which additional finance may reach schools.

The first is by donations from PTAs or similar organisations. The head and governors have no responsibility for the raising of funds by such bodies since they are independent organisations though, of course, they could disapprove of any methods used or refuse to allow the premises to be used for particular events. Once a PTA has donated money to a school then the school becomes responsible for its security and proper accounting. Perhaps the best approach is for the PTA not to donate money at all but to purchase specific items of equipment which have been approved by the school as suitable and necessary. This helps with the school's budget and avoids the need for additional accounting. It also gives parents the undoubted pleasure of seeing the tangible rewards of their efforts.

Secondly, there may be a trust fund linked to the school, especially if it has a religious foundation. Responsibility here lies with the trustees who must act in accordance with the deed of trust, only granting finance for items allowed for under that deed. The head or governors may give advice to the trustees, or refuse to accept their proposals, but that is all.

Insurance

Insurance is a form of contract. The insured pays a premium and, in return, the insurance company promises to pay out certain sums in the event of certain happenings. Insurance contracts are said to be of utmost good faith which means that the person or body seeking insurance cover must reveal all relevant details or the contract will be invalid.

When entering into insurance contracts there needs to be a careful check as to what the contract covers — and what it does not — and the amounts payable if a claim is made. These amounts may not be sufficient, and there will certainly be exclusion clauses and excess charges in a number of categories.

Schools must have insurance and the main types are as follows.

Financial matters

Building and contents

Grant-maintained and aided schools must take out their own. For other schools, the LEA may decide to pay all insurance costs and reflect this in the school's delegated budget allowance or it may cater for this in the allowance and require schools to make their own arrangements. Some authorities insure for major issues such as fire, explosion and subsidence but leave governors responsible for events such as theft or vandalism. Each school needs to check on its own position.

Public and employer's liability

As we saw earlier, employers are vicariously liable for the actions of employees — not their crimes though — while in the performance of their duties, so insurance to cover liability for the negligence of employees is compulsory. This would cover a pupil's claim that an injury was caused by inadequate supervision by staff or that equipment had not been used properly or safely. Equally, it could cover a claim by a member of staff that an injury had been caused by some defect in the premises or school equipment.

There is also a need to have insurance against claims by any third party that the school's negligence has caused harm, e.g. damage caused by pupils on a visit, even though the supervision had been adequate.

Money

It is likely that insurance will cover theft of official monies collected in school — dinner money, for example — but is there cover for money given as a voluntary contribution, or towards a school visit, or in the possession of employees? This position needs to be clarified and additional insurance cover obtained.

Personal accident

Some schools believe that, if a pupil is injured, there is automatic cover by insurance. This is not so in the vast majority of schools. The insurance company will only pay out if there is negligence and this may not exist or may be difficult to prove. A pupil injured in a

126 Legal issues and the self-managing school

properly conducted sporting activity would provide a good example. Any compensation would be extremely unlikely.

Insurance against personal accident is well worthwhile since it would also cover accidents outside school but the school is under no obligation to provide it, and the cost of doing so for all pupils would be prohibitive. Parents should be made aware of this lack of cover and encouraged to take out personal accident insurance for their children, either individually or through a joint scheme sponsored by the school or perhaps by the PTA.

Personal accident cover should always be included in any major school visit, and reputable school journey associations will include this as part of the package. Again, the extent of the cover and any exclusions need to be checked.

Contracts

Grant-maintained and aided schools make their own contracts. While other schools may make the initial contacts and discuss terms, the actual contract as yet is between the contractor and the LEA. This position may very well change. Schools therefore need to study the terms of any contract very carefully and know what action to take if a contractor fails in his obligations.

Business contracts are always assumed to be legally binding unless clearly stated to be otherwise. Evidence of the agreement needs to be available so the contract is always best expressed in writing.

Incident

A joiner is contracted to repair a bank of school lockers and a price is agreed. The work is carried out badly so that doors will not close and some drop off at the slightest touch. The school refuses to pay for the job and the joiner threatens legal action.

The school could certainly refuse to pay. The joiner is in default of a basic condition in the contract, that the work shall be carried out in a professional and suitable manner. A claim could be lodged against the joiner in the small claims section of the local county court for the cost of paying someone else to put matters right.

This court may be used for speedy settlement where relatively small sums are involved. The procedure is informal, the cost low, and legal representation is not necessary.

Financial matters 127

Summary

Governors are responsible for school policies over finance. These include proper arrangements for the collection, recording, accounting, security and auditing of both official and unofficial funds. Such policies must be in accord with any relevant legislation and, in the case of voluntary and county schools, with the LMS scheme that is in force. Governors must also guard against serious financial claims by taking out appropriate insurance.

14 Records, references and copyright

George Orwell's predictions for 1984 may not have materialised to the extent that he imagined but many have the feeling that information regarding themselves exists of which they are unaware and over which they have little control. Anyone who has suffered because of errors in credit ratings knows how worrying and damaging that can be. Nevertheless, recording of data is always necessary for many useful and innocent purposes, and the requirements for schools to do so have certainly increased under the extended autonomy and delegation of powers.

Terence is a pupil and Horace is a teacher. Here is a list of possible records that might apply to each in their involvement at school.

Terence
Birth certificate
Entry on admissions register
Entry on class register
Report to juvenile court
Report to family court
Report to social services
Entry on at-risk register for abuse
Statement of special educational needs
School report to parents
School leaving reference

Horace

Entry on DFE records as a qualified teacher
Employer's records of personal details and service
School-based records on personal file
Appraisal statement
References for job applications

Records, references and copyright 129

While some of these may not seem to raise legal issues — birth certificates are public documents and available for inspection by anyone — many others raise problems relating to recording, security and confidentiality, and these have become more complex with the widespread use of computers. This has led to the passing of the Data Protection Act.

Data protection

The Data Protection Act of 1984 has the aim of protecting individuals against the misuse of personal data stored by automatic means. Those who do store data by such means are required by law to register as users with the Data Protection Registrar, Wycliffe House, Water Lane, Wilmslow, Cheshire SK9 5AF. Since LEAs will now keep employee records on computer, they must register as users. This registration would cover voluntary and county schools where the data were collected on behalf of the LEA, say for transmission to the DFE — attendance records would be an example. If these schools store other data on computer, as almost certainly they will do, then they too must register as users. Aided and grant-maintained schools will have to register anyway.

Under the terms of registration, the user must only store data relevant and adequate for the user's purpose and these must be removed when they are no longer of use. The data must be kept securely, and access to them must be limited, so staff should not have open access. That is where problems for schools may lie.

Any person who believes that data are being kept regarding himslf or herself may make a request in writing to the user and a fee may be charged. The user must be satisfied as to the identity of the applicant, and the application must be by the person concerned. If parents ask for data relating to a pupil then the pupil must authorise this specifically. Of course, parents have a right to access to data regarding themselves as a family, so the distinction may sometimes be dificult. The admissions register, for example, records data on Terence and on all who have parental responsibility under the new Children Act.

Must all data stored on computer be accessible in this way? One exception which may affect schools is that of medical information which might be held to cause serious harm or concern to the subject. Problems remain over access to court reports and entry on the at-risk register. Since the Act does not apply to records made and stored by manual means, the recording of highly sensitive information might best be recorded by such means rather than by computer. That does not relieve the school of the need for careful and accurate recording, secure keeping and a concern for confidentiality.

130 Legal issues and the self-managing school

Guidelines from the DFE suggest that the following are suitable for storage by schools on computer and for which the head or governing body should be registered as a user:

1. Admission and attendance registers.
2. Curricular records of pupils, including details of exemptions from the National Curriculum.
3. Details of assessments made under the National Curriculum.
4. Entries for prescribed public examinations such as GCSE and their results.
5. Reports on the progress of their children.
6. Staff records. The DFE includes appraisal statements, which seems tactless advice in view of staff feelings on this aspect.
7. Records of pupils relating to disciplinary action.
8. Records of dealings with contractors.

The governors would be users under 1, 2, 4, 6 and 8 for aided and grant-maintained schools and others where records dealt with expenditure outside the delegated budget. The head would be the user under 3, 5, 7 and under 6 if appraisal statements were included.

Confidentiality

Whether stored automatically or not, almost all the records relating to Terence and Horace raise problems of confidentiality.

Names and addresses of parents from the admission register may be given to candidates standing for election as parent governors and who wish to circulate a statement to other parents. With perhaps some reluctance, these could also be released to the police — who could obtain a warrant anyway — if a crime is under investigation. There may be a case for releasing them to aid social services enquiries or those by the NSPCC in extreme situations, but schools should not make them freely available.

Court reports should be kept confidential though certainly at juvenile hearings those affected will either have to be shown the school's report or made aware of its contents. A normal school report is confidential to pupil and parents and, in the case of an 18-year-old, confidential to the pupil. An 'at-risk' register relating to suspected abuse, and to any reports relating to it, are confidential to the school and the head will have to make the difficult decision as to which staff shall have access to this register and to the details it contains.

Appraisal statements of staff are confidential to the head, the appraiser if not the head, and to the subject. Governors have no right

Records, references and copyright 131

of access though the chair has a right to see the statement relating to the head. References relating to staff or pupils may be open or confidential. If open, they should be passed to the subject of the reference who will then be responsible for their use. If confidential, there needs to be a clear understanding of what that means, i.e. is the subject to be made aware of the contents or only the person towards whom the reference is addressed?

All this means that the head must give careful thought to who collects data, where they are to be stored, and who will have access to it. The role of office staff in handling sensitive information needs to be examined. The school office is normally a very busy place with staff and other visitors coming and going. Even a trustworthy secretary having to deal with confidential matters in such an environment may have difficulty in defeating the curious. The secretary needs some privacy when dealing with such matters.

References, reports and defamation

Earlier in this book we explained the law relating to discrimination, how in interviews certain questions must not be allowed, and how discriminatory treatment of staff and pupils must be avoided in other matters. A similar approach is needed in the writing of reports and references.

The writing of reports and references is a common task in schools, and a second problem with them may be the risk of an accusation of defamation of character. Yet, unless references in particular are frank they are likely to be of little value and, indeed, if they deliberately hide relevant known facts the writers may even be negligent. The fear of uttering defamatory statements, however, is a very real one and so a basic understanding of the law is helpful to give confidence and avoid pitfalls.

Defamation is the making of an untrue statement about another to third parties which lowers the reputation of that person in the eyes of respectable and right-thinking persons. Who they might be is a matter for the court to decide and juries may well, in effect, have to decide this in defamation cases.

There are two types of defamation: libel and slander. Libel is defamation in a permanent form, and all writing falls into that category, even that on a blackboard which might easily be rubbed out. Recordings on video or cassette could constitute libel and so could drawings or photographs. References and reports clearly fall into this category. Slander is defamation in an impermanent form, usually speech, though a gesture might qualify.

132   Legal issues and the self-managing school

The difference between them can be important in law. In a suit for libel, the plaintiff does not have to prove damage, only the lowering of reputation. In slander, damage does have to be proved, though for teachers there is an important exception. Slandering a person's reputation in his professional capacity does not require proof of damage, that goes without saying.

Mr Smith

He had applied for another teaching post. An extract from the head's confidential reference read:

> Mr Smith is a competent teacher who has good relationships with most pupils and colleagues. He does, however, have a quick temper and is apt to lose this occasionally with difficult pupils, when he is prone to swear at them. There have been parental complaints and Mr Smith has been warned as to his conduct in this respect. He is genuinely sorry when such incidents occur.

This could be libel since the statement is in written form. The head has two possible defences should Mr Smith discover what has been said and threaten to sue. First, that of justification — the statement is true (we assume that it is so). Secondly, that of what is known as qualified privilege. When a person is under obligation to provide a reference, and heads can be required to do so, their remarks are protected by privilege unless it can be shown that they were made with malice. The head here appears to have been honest but if there had been just one incident and no complaints then malice would certainly have been present.

Mr Jones

He is another one who swears at pupils. The head hears him do this in the corridor and calls him to his office after school. Tempers become heated. The head ends by telling Mr Jones that he is a disgrace to the profession, and Mr Jones responds by saying that the head is an incompetent ass who knows nothing of the strain under which his staff have to work.

Both these statements could amount to slander. However, neither person could take legal action over this since a defamatory statement must be communicated to a third party and this has not happened — the head, of course, could have taken disciplinary action over the swearing. If an inquisitive secretary had been listening at an open door then communication would have taken place — publishing is the legal term — and each would have a right of action against the other. Neither would have to prove damage because, in both cases, the slur is on professional reputation.

The defamation may be of a pupil.

Records, references and copyright 133

> **Terence again**
>
> Part of his form tutor's summary on his report included the following:
>
> Terence is a boy of considerable intelligence and does well in mathematics and science, as this report indicates, because he is interested. In other subjects his efforts are spasmodic and there seems little doubt that with greater efforts he could do better. I'm afraid that in class he tends to be disruptive and around the school he has bullied younger pupils and taken sweets and money from them.

There is a serious accusation here — that Terence is a thief. The teacher needs to be able to substantiate this without any doubt whatsoever or an action for libel could certainly lie. If this were untrue, others would certainly think badly of him and the statement has been published to parents.

Some readers might think that a teacher would not write such a comment on a pupil's report but, during his time as a head, the writer came across a number of similar incidents. The school needs to have some form of checking the wording of reports before they go to parents to prevent bad feeling and embarrassment and tactfully require teachers to alter statements that could be defamatory. This does not mean that reports should not be frank.

Defamation by parents or others

What if defamatory statements are made of the head, members of staff or the governors?

> **Parents' annual meeting**
>
> The meeting was well attended because of a wide concern over the teaching of mathematics in the school. Tempers began to rise and at one stage an angry parent exclaimed:
>
> This man Newton can't control kids and he can't teach maths. Seems to spend all his time in the class playing with apples. You governors are supposed to be responsible for this school and its teachers. You're not doing your job, you're incompetent. And you, chairman, are just ducking the issue by not letting us talk about Newton.

The chairman, of course, was behaving correctly in not allowing the meeting to discuss personalities, though the governors might have promised with the head to look into the teaching of mathematics in the school.

134 Legal issues and the self-managing school

The statement regarding Mr Newton is capable of amounting to slander. It has been published and reflects upon his professional ability. However, the law of defamation is not intended to stifle genuine criticism of those with authority and public responsibility. The parent would have the defence of fair comment on a matter of public interest as far as the governing body was concerned and possibly with regard to Mr Newton. Whether it is fair or not is an open question.

Fair comment is the defence commonly used by the media. The recent court decision in the action by Derbyshire CC against *Times* Newspapers that public bodies cannot sue in defamation means that the governing body could take no action, even if it has a legal entity through incorporation. Individual governors who were defamed could certainly do so if statements referred to them personally.

Copyright

> **Cats**
> A school is staging a production of this work in order to raise funds for new stage lighting. Copies of the script and music are expensive and in order to save money one copy of each is obtained and further copies for the cast and organisers run off on the school's photocopying machine. The English department sees a good chance here to link this to some study of T.S. Eliot's works in class. Photocopies are made of several poems for class use and one copy is made of a particular poem on a slide for an OHP to be shown to a class for a discussion period. An extract of some hundred words is copied from an Eliot essay on literary criticism for use with an A-Level group, and they will also be shown a video recording of a BBC programme on the life of the poet.

There are clear breaches of copyright here but some uses which may be legitimate.

Copyright is a form of property. It lies in the right to control the use of original work in literary, dramatic, musical and artistic works. It does not lie in the ideas themselves but in the form in which those ideas are expressed. It is automatic, owners do not have to register their claim. The work does not have to have any great worth or significance — a pupil's story printed in a school magazine has just as much right as a work by a famous author. Copyright does not lie in ordinary factual material which has no stamp of originality about it.

Copyright is a part of the civil law — unlike data protection which is criminal — and the remedies for breach are compensation in the form of money damages or an injunction to prevent further copying. It has always been a complicated area of the law because of the

Records, references and copyright

difficulty of discovery and this has been exacerbated by the wide use of photocopiers, cassettes, compact discs and videos.

The Copyright, Designs and Patents Act 1988 has attempted to bring the law more in line with modern conditions and has created a Copyright Tribunal to deal with disputes, but the old law may well apply to works created before that date. A further complication is that a single work may involve more than one copyright owner and a cassette or compact disc provides a good example. There may be copyright in the composer, the lyricist, the group playing the music and the agency which made the recording. Also, in any one work one copyright may have expired while another still exists. The copyright of a novel by Dickens has expired so far as his heirs are concerned but the copyright of the typesetting of a new edition of his novel still remains with the publisher.

Normally, copyright lasts for 50 years from the death of the original owner and, like other forms of property, may be left by will. For published editions it lasts for 25 years.

In recent years, there have been several successful actions against schools for breach of copyright and it must be said that, in spite of the publicity thus gained, there is still misunderstanding of the law and breach of it. Schools need to be aware of the copying that is permitted:

- That by permission of the owner, whether a fee is charged or not. Some suppliers now include a right to copy as part of the package that they sell.
- That where it can be shown that reasonable attempts to find the owner have failed.
- That of copies for research or private study — this is known as fair dealing.
- That of a relatively insignificant part of a large work — a page from a novel, for example, but not a quatrain from a sonnet.
- The making of a single copy for instruction.
- That of a 'reasonable proportion' of a published work for research or private study.
- That for examination purposes — that does not include music.
- Performing in public extracts from literary or dramatic works, providing an acknowledgement is given.
- Copying under licence.

These are not rights but concessions. The copyright owner could stipulate that they do not apply in the particular instance.

Licences

The licensing of the public performance of music has been in existence for some time through the Performing Rights Society. An annual fee covers performance, and most LEAs deal with this on behalf of schools. A record of the music used is usually required.

In an effort to ease problems over copyright, a new additional system of licensing has been set up and the two bodies concerned are of particular importance for schools.

The Copyright Licensing Agency

Licensing may be direct or through the LEA and the terms of the licence must be displayed beside the machines used for copying so that users understand them. The licence allows the copying of up to 5 per cent of any work published by the Agency, and most major publishers are members. The scheme covers mechanical and electronic copying but music is not included. A fee is payable.

The Educational Recording Agency

This agency was set up as a result of the 1988 Act. For a single annual fee, schools may copy programmes produced by members of the agency which includes the BBC and ITA, though not the Open University. Any other copying of programmes is breach of copyright.

Cats

If we turn again to the production mentioned earlier, we find that the school is in breach of copyright over the copying of script and music. It will also be in breach over the playing of the music in public unless there is a current licence from the Performing Rights Society or from the agent handling the production rights. There is a breach in copying a number of copies of poems for class use but not in producing one copy on an OHP for class discussion. The short extract from the Eliot essay would be permissible and so would the showing of the BBC programme, provided that the school was registered with the Educational Recording Agency.

The basic rule over copyright is, of course, to contact the owner of the rights if there is any doubt.

Summary

When storing data or copying material, schools need to be aware of the provisions of the Data Protection Act and the Copyright Act. As far as

Records, references and copyright 137

data is concerned, whether on computer or not, accuracy, security and confidentiality are of utmost importance and must be planned for. Those writing reports or references on others need to be frank and honest but they need to be sure that they can justify any remarks which cast a shadow on the reputation of those others.

Further reading

General

The Law of Education Liell and Sanders, Butterworths Loose-leaf in three files.
The Head's Legal Guide Croner. Loose-leaf file.
The English Legal System K. Eddey, Sweet and Maxwell, 1987.

Governing bodies

Your own Instrument and Articles of Government.

School Governors: A Guide to the Law DFE, 1992.
The School Governor's Legal Guide C. Lowe, Croner, 1993.
Governor's Handbook Ace.
School Governors: How to Become a Grant-maintained School DFE, 1992.

Employment

Tolley's Employment Handbook E. A. Slade, Tolley, 1993.
The Burgundy Book — Conditions of Service for Schoolteachers in England and Wales loose-leaf, from LEAs.
The Blue Book — Schoolteachers' Pay and Conditions Document HMSO. Issued annually.

Your own disciplinary and grievance procedures

Fair and Unfair Dismissal HMSO, booklet, 1987.
School Teacher Appraisal DFE circular 12/91.

Further reading

Parents and pupils

Family Law and Practice Reekie and Tuddenham, Sweet and Maxwell, 1990.
School Management and Pupil Behaviour N. Jones, Falmer, 1989.
Amendment of pupils registration regulations 1956: keeping of school records DFE memorandum 1/88.
Introduction to the Children Act HMSO, 1989.
Special Education Handbook Ace.

Premises and health and safety

Education (School Premises) Regulations 1981 Statutory Instrument 909.
Health and Safety in Schools B. Stock, Croner, 1993.
Safety in Outdoor Education; Safety at School: General Advice; Safety in Science Laboratories; Safety in Practical Studies; Safety in Physical Education. All booklets available from DFE.
Public Entertainment Licensing and School Premises Home Office, 1984.

Finance

Managing School Finance B. Knight, Heinemann, 1983.
Local Financial Management in Schools P. Downes, Blackwell, 1988.
Local Management of Schools B. Davies and C. Braund, Northcote House, 1989.
Education Reform Act 1988. Charges for School Activities DFE circular 2/89.

Negligence and defamation

Tort C. D. Baker, Sweet and Maxwell, 1991.

Data protection

Guidelines from the Registrar, 1989.

Copyright

Copyright Clearance Guide National Council for Educational Technology.

Addresses

Advisory Centre for Education, 18 Victoria Park Square, London E2 9PB.

Association of Teachers and Lecturers, 7 Northumberland Street, London WC2N 5DA.

Catholic Education Services, 41 Cromwell Road, London SW7 2DH.

Charity Commissioners, St Alban's House, 57–60 Haymarket, London SW1 4QX, or Graeme House, Derby Square, Liverpool L2 7SB.

Commission for Racial Equality, Elliott House, 10–12 Allington Street, London SW1E 5EH.

Council for Education Technology, 3 Devonshire Stret, London W1N 2BA.

Data Protection Registrar, Wycliffe House, Water Lane, Wilmslow, Cheshire SK9 5AF.

Department for Education, Sanctuary Buildings, Great Smith Street, Westminster, London SW1P 3BT.

Department for Education, Publications Despatch Centre, Honeypot Lane, Stanmore, Middlesex HA7 1AZ.

Educational Recording Agency, 33–34 Alfred Place, London WC1E 7DP.

Employment Appeal Tribunal, 4 St James's Square, London SW1Y 4JU.

Equal Opportunities Commission, Overseas House, Quay Street, Manchester M3 3HN.

General Synod Board of Education, Church House, Great Smith Street, London SW1P 3NZ.

Grant-Maintained Schools Centre, Wesley Court, 4a Priory Road, High Wycombe, Buckinghamshire HP13 6SE.

Health and Safety Executive, St Hugh's House, Stanley Precinct, Bootle, Merseyside L20 3QZ.

Addresses 141

Her Majesty's Stationery Office, Publications Centre, PO Box 276, London SW8 5DT.

National Association of Governors and Managers, Suite 36/38, 21 Bennetts Hill, Birmingham B2 5QP.

National Association of Head Teachers, 1 Heath Square, Boltro Road, Haywards Heath, West Sussex RH16 1BL.

National Association of Schoolmasters/Union of Women Teachers, Hillscourt Educational Centre, Rose Hill, Rednal, Birmingham B45 8RS.

National Confederation of Parent–Teacher Associations, 2 Ebbsfleet Industrial Estate, 43 Stonebridge Road, Gravesend, Kent DA11 9DZ.

National Curriculum Council, Albion Wharf, 25 Skeldergate, York YO1 2XL.

National Society for the Prevention of Cruelty to Children, 67 Saffron Hill, London EC1N 8RS.

National Union of Teachers, Hamilton House, Mabledon Place, London WC1H 9DB.

Office for Standards in Education, Sanctuary Buildings, Great Smith Street, London SW2P 3BT.

Professional Association of Teachers, 2 St James Court, Friargate, Derby DE1 1BT.

Safety and First Aid, 59 Hill Street, Liverpool L8 5SA.

School Examinations and Assessment Council, Newcombe House, 45 Notting Hill Gate, London W11 3JB.

Secondary Heads Association, 130 Regent Road, Leicester LE1 7PG.

Universities Central Council on Admissions, PO Box 28, Cheltenham, Gloucestershire GL50 3SA.

Index

Acts of Parliament, 2, 4, 6
agenda, 31
appraisal, 46
Articles of Government, 8
attendance, 3, 68
 registers and, 71

bullying, 84

case law, 6
cases,
 Crump v Gilmore 1969, 2
 Hinchley v Ranking 1961, 2
 Jenkins v Howell 1969, 2
 Mandla v Dowel Lee 1983, 51
chair of governors,
 action by, 33
charging, 121
conditions of service, 44
confidentiality, 130
contracts, 12, 126
 of insurance, 124
 of service, 40
copyright, 15, 134
crime, 14
 pupils and, 95

data protection, 16, 129
defamation, 131
DFE circulars, 3, 8
detention, 92
directed time, 47
discipline,
 and pastoral care, 87
 and suspension of staff, 55
 of employees, 52
 rules and, 88
 warnings and, 53

employment law, 10
exclusion, 92
external agencies, 84

family law, 13

finance, 120
 unofficial funds, 123
 visits and, 123
fire drill, 114
first aid, 115

governors,
 annual report by, 36
 appointment of, 26
 charging by, 121
 committees of, 29, 34
 contracts by, 121
 election of, 27
 health and safety and, 111
 ineligibility of, 27
 meetings of, 31
 parent, 28
 teacher, 29
grievance procedures, 58

heads,
 powers of, 22
 reports by, 33
health and safety, 11, 110
 assessment of risks, 112
 committee for, 111
 reports and, 113
 safety representatives, 111

in loco parentis, 97
Instrument of Government, 8
insurance, 124
interviews, 43

job descriptions, 41

licensing, 117, 135
lotteries, 118

meetings, 15, 31
 confidentiality of, 35
 minutes of, 32
 withdrawal from, 34
minibuses, 16, 122

Index

143

negligence, 103, 108

occupier's liability, 17, 108

parents,
  annual meeting for, 36
  attendance and, 68
  duties of, 67
  information for, 75
  rights of, 74
  school rules and, 72
pastoral care, 81
  bullying and, 84
  discipline and, 87
  external agencies and, 87
premises, 17, 106
  licencing and, 117
  trespass and, 118
  use by outside bodies, 122
PTAs, 79
pupils,
  admission of, 74
  attendance by, 68
  detention of, 92
  exclusion of, 92
  special needs of, 78
  supervision of, 97
  use of force on, 95
  violence by, 95

records, 129
redundancy, 63

registers, 71
rules, 88
  dress and, 91
  legal force of, 91

sanctions, 91

schools,
  county, 25
  grant-maintained, 27, 37
  special agreement, 27
  visits by, 102, 123
  voluntary aided, 27
  voluntary controlled, 25
Secretary of State, 21
staff,
  discipline of, 52
  dismissal of, 121
  suspension of, 55
  warnings to, 53
Statutory instruments, 2, 6
supervision, 97
  duties and, 99
  off premises, 101

tort, 13
trespass, 108, 118
tribunals, 15
  remedies by, 65